OUR SI-FI GOD

OUR SI-FI GOD

GENEVA HEWETT

gatekeeper press™

Columbus, Ohio

Our Si-Fi God

Published by Gatekeeper Press

2167 Stringtown Rd, Suite 109

Columbus, OH 43123-2989

www.GatekeeperPress.com

Library of Congress Control Number: 2020950037

ISBN (paperback): 9781662905766

eISBN: 9781662905773

CONTENTS

ANOTHER SI-FI MOMENT

While I was on vacation in New Smyrna Beach, Florida, my husband and I were sitting on the beach and watching the sunrise. As the sun continued to rise, it began to form something that blew us away. The clouds began to form shapes that appeared as angels' wings — huge angels' wings. It wasn't until the sun popped over the horizon and fell right smack in between the wings that we realized it formed the head of the angel. Beams of light pierced through the morning skylight that radiated the whole body of the angel. Chills came all over my body as we experienced this marvelous handiwork of Almighty God. What a spectacular gift we witnessed on this morning that was set aside not only for us but for those who were blessed enough to witness it with us. The Lord shows up in the most unusual places if you have an eye to see. Always be looking for Him. He is ever present.

Geneva

Our Si-Fi God

By Geneva Hewett

Crazy name for a book? Not really.

Just take a look and you will see that this book will expose you to the many faces of Jesus and the many ways he shows up in our lives.

This book will empower you as you read the short stories, the parables, and the testimonies of the Lord. He is alive and constantly working on our behalf that we all may be overcomers, so we can tell others about his marvelous works.

Revelation 12:11

And they overcame him (the devil) by the blood of the lamb and by the word of their testimony, and they loved not their lives unto the death. (KJV)

Acknowledgments

Of course it goes without saying that I thank my precious Lord and Savior for being my closest friend. Without Him talking to me, giving me dreams and visions and eyes to see what the spirit is really saying, there would be no story to tell. I have a story to tell because He wants us all to see the greatness of His love for us and He longs to be in every aspect of our lives. Our everyday walk with Him is so vital. He is the air we breathe and the songs we sing. Thank you, Lord, for sharing your many personalities with me through the stories you blessed me with.

Oh, my goodness, how very much I want to thank my wonderful husband Leon Hewett for the Christ-like patience he has shown me through our marriage of thirty-nine years. I came to him with a lot of baggage, and he has so graciously helped me walk through the deep hurts and pains I encountered early in life. He has encouraged me to complete this book as a testimony of how great our God is as our deliverer and healer. He has always listened to my Si-Fi stories and even encouraged me to always be sensitive to the Lord. He loves the way the Lord speaks to me and has reminded me often how precious and powerful that gift is. He constantly reminds me to stay close under the shadow of God's wing so I may hear clearly what the Spirit is saying.

I also want to express my thanks to my prayer partners — we call ourselves the fabulous four. We have helped one another through many of life's trying times, yet we always find the time to relish each other's accomplishments. Thank you, Carrie, Leisa, and Kathy, for always being there for me. Special thanks to Carrie George for challenging to me write this book and to never give up, because I wanted to give up more than once. You are a Godly inspiration to us all, Carrie.

Thank you my children, because you have walked through many of these stories with me. You were also patient and kind at a time when I was unlovable. May God bestow upon you the sweetest mercies that you have so graciously bestowed upon me. Boys, you have taught me as much as I have ever taught you, and I am still learning from you. I love you so very much, Clint, Todd, and Andy.

Rhonda, thank you for being a dear friend who has shared so many God encounters with me. It has been amazing to see how God orchestrated His divine timing in so many situations for His perfect will to be accomplished when we least expected it. I love how we would always say, "OK, what's God up to now?" We always knew it would stretch us and we loved it. I know you have had my back through thick and thin, just as I have had yours. May we always be there for each other, keep our eyes on Jesus, and stay the course.

WELCOME TO THE Si-Fi ZONE OF GOD

By Geneva Hewett

TRUE GOD ENCOUNTERS THAT WILL INSPIRE YOU AS YOU LAUGH, CRY, AND PRAISE GOD FOR LETTING HIM BE A PART OF YOUR EVERYDAY LIFE.

Welcome to the Si-Fi zone of God, where anything is possible, and where the Bible truly comes to life in our everyday walk with Jesus. Wow! Think about all the fascinating stories in the Bible. Are you not just blown away? It is filled with the natural and supernatural — stories you almost can't believe because they are so out there. Our God is a God of signs and wonders, always showing Himself to us in the most unusual ways. He shows up at the most unexpected times, wowing us with how He speaks and shows us His heart in the lessons He longs to reveal to us. He loves being with us on a daily basis to speak to us if we allow Him to. Every time I would have an encounter with the Lord, I would say, "Wow, that was cool." After a while I realized it was more than cool; I thought these special moments were actually so uniquely unusual I began to call them Si-Fi God moments. From that moment on I have called them my Si- Fi God encounters. This is not science fiction; it is just a play on words. Si-Fi in this book means these encounters are radical moments in time where only God could have set each circumstance or event.

These special moments in time are addictive. They cause you to long to be in His presence. They cause you to see beyond what you are looking at in the natural and see what God may be showing you through the lens of His eyes. You realize you were born for more than taking up air space. You were born to see and hear the mysteries of God. You were born to serve. You were born to create. You were born to minister. You were born to have dominion over this Earth. Wow, I get excited just thinking about it!

Isn't it wonderful to walk in an awareness that He is always near and that He longs to reveal Himself to us even more than we long to be with Him? Now is the season for all of us to share our encounters with the world as a testimony of how great our Lord is. Let everything that has breath praise the Lord. Let us all be free in Christ. Whom the Son has set free is free indeed.

This book contains testimonies about the random times God showed up and wanted to speak in a way only He can express Himself. God has a way of revealing truth through many avenues. Let us be in awe of how creative He is, as we learn to see Him in the unique ways He shows himself to us. Every story in this book is so unique because He never does the same thing twice to teach me lessons. All the encounters you will read are true, and I am privileged to share them with you. My heart's desire in sharing this book is so you, too, can see God and how He works in our everyday lives to advance the Kingdom. He uses us as individuals as a testimony of how He works through people like you and me. His desire is that all people would be drawn to Him by whatever avenue it takes. Use this book as a devotion book, a teaching tool, or an inspirational book to just read and soak in the goodness of God.

I encourage you to expect the unexpected. Expect the impossible. Look beyond the natural into the supernatural. Never put God in a box. Stop limiting Him with our small view of how we think He is and how He operates. When you do you just might have your own encounter with the King of Kings and the Lord of Lords. Who knows what is right around the corner? I want excitement to fill your heart as you yield to the Holy Spirit and let Him do His job, which is to teach you all things.

Open your heart as you enjoy the journey, not into the Twilight Zone, but into the Si-Fi zone of God.

Let's get in the zone!

TOTALLY UNJUSTIFIED

SOMETIMES LIFE ISN'T FAIR

I was about twelve years old when this story took place. It is a story I have shared with only a few people in my life; however, I feel like it needs to be told, because I know many of you have gone through similar experiences. Maybe we do not share these experiences because they bring up the past, and for many the past is better left buried. I chose to share my story because it may bring healing to those who read it and let them know they are not the only person that has been treated unjustly.

Growing up, we learned at an early age to never cross our mother. That means we walked on eggshells. We did just about anything to please her because we knew what would happen if we did not. We as children were responsible for most of the chores around the house and for seeing to our other siblings. That was fine because we all knew our roles, and everything ran like a well-oiled machine.

Let me tell you a little about my mother through my eyes. She was an extremely beautiful woman. She could do anything. She could multitask better than anyone I have ever seen. She was as good at tending to things on the outside of the house as well as on the inside. There was nothing she tackled that she could not do. She could play a guitar. She could kill and clean a deer and then make sausage from that deer. She could plow a field and then replant it with the crop that was needed for the next season. She canned all of our garden vegetables and cooked the greatest meals you ever put in your mouth. I could go on and on, but you get the picture. I looked up to her in so many ways. There was only one problem. She was a mean, controlling woman. That in itself took away all the good I saw. For that very reason, I did not want to be like her.

In her second marriage, my mother was married to a man in the Navy, and he was stationed on an aircraft carrier. He was my stepfather. While he was away for a couple of months on duty, she began to see another man. He was at our home frequently. He spent the night a couple nights a week. He would be there when we got up and when we got in from school. We all went to the beach together, so he naturally became part of our everyday routine. We thought this was strange, but of course we would never question anything she did — that would be a no-no. Instead, we just talked about it among ourselves as siblings. You know the old hush-hush rule.

The time had finally come for my stepfather to come back into town from his duty on board ship, so needless to say we did not see the boyfriend anymore. Everything went back to the way it was before the boyfriend left. Although we did notice there seemed to be more tension and fussing, we stayed out of our parents' arguments. After about a week or so my mother came to the school one day for no apparent reason to pick me up. Back then they called you over the intercom system. The lady said over the intercom, "Geneva, will you please come to the office? Your mother is here to pick you up." I wondered why she would be picking me up from school because I did not have any doctor's appointment and she never let us get out of school for anything. I was puzzled and I felt like something was up but could not figure it out.

Mother pulled up to the front of the school and I got in the car. I could sense something was wrong immediately. There was such a strong silence for about five minutes. I asked her why she was picking me up and I asked her if everything was all right. After a few minutes she responded with a loud stern voice, saying, "You little bitch! You did this on purpose." I had no clue as to what she was referring to. I said, "What are you talking about?"

I was scared out of my pants. She told me that I just wanted to stir trouble and that I knew exactly what I was doing. I kept asking what she was referring to, because I honestly had no clue as to what on Earth she was talking about. She finally told me I had called my stepdad her boyfriend's name on purpose and now she was in trouble with my stepdad. She said, "That's OK, you are going to pay." I got so scared. What did she mean? I was going to pay. Where was she taking me? If I had called my stepfather her boyfriend's name, I certainly did not do it on purpose. Heck, he was around for almost two months. It may have slipped. I don't remember.

I would never cross her path and do such a crazy thing. I was a lot smarter than that. She continued to imply over and over that I had done this on purpose. I was crying, and I told her I did not do this on purpose, and if I did let it slip accidentally, I was sorry. Nothing I said was working because she already had her mind made up and she was on a mission — one that I was not privy to. We kept driving in a direction I was not familiar with, so I did not know where we would end up.

The next thing I knew we were driving down a dirt road. We pulled off onto a small side road and she cut the car off. She told me to get out of the car. I did. At this point I was shaking because the one thing I knew about mother was that I was going to get a beating. This was her MO. I watched her walk towards the woods, and she began to break off some huge switches from the nearby shrubs. Some of them were as big as my pointer finger. They looked like sticks. As she started back, she told me to strip down to nothing. I had to take everything off. I was crying so hard, but I knew it would not help. Sometimes it made it worse. After I stripped down, she proceeded to whip me with the switches, and not gently, either. She was taking her anger out on me. She started at my shoulders and went all the way down to my ankles. She mostly stayed on my back because it was less detectable to the teachers at school. After what seemed like a lifetime of her whipping and cursing at me and accusing me unjustly, she stopped. She told me to put my clothes back on and for me to never think I could get away with exposing her like I did. I said nothing. I got into the car with blood coming down my back onto my clothes. It hurt so badly, but I would not say a word.

She kept me out of school for the next three days so no one could see the marks on my body. We had gone to school with marks on us before and she was called in by the principal, so she got wise to that and would keep us out of school until we healed. I was assigned to cleaning baseboards, scrubbing floors, pulling weeds out of the flowerbeds, and anything else to keep me busy as my punishment. I cannot remember where my stepfather was. I think he had left for a few days. I just did what I was told, and I did not murmur or complain.

Was this an unjust thing that happened to me? Absolutely. Over my life I have replayed this whole scene over and over. It has always been a painful story to think about and share. I felt like my mother hated me. I think it seemed like all of us children were just in her way. I guess we all felt like we would all be better off if we ran away or were taken from her. It wasn't until later on in life I had peace over the whole ordeal. I will share with you what came to me as I processed my experience in the woods: Bad things happen to good people, and even to children.

- How can we ever think we may not have to endure hardships just as Christ did?

- As I replayed this scene, I thought of Christ. He was beaten beyond recognition, and He was innocent, just like me.

- It made me appreciate the cross more than if I had not experienced this abuse.

- Every story I have written I have experienced. This enables me to minister in a whole new dimension. I can now minister with a real passion of love and forgiveness.

- John 16:33 says in this world you will have trouble, but take heart, because I have overcome the world. Yes, we will go through hard things, and we pray no one else will ever have to endure such experiences, but if we do, we can be overcomers. It will be part of our journey that will only make us stronger — stronger to love on others.

My prayer for anyone who is reading this story and who has been through any traumatic event is that you use your experience to grow in your personal walk with Jesus Christ, as well as using it as a tool to minister to others. We cannot teach in fullness what we do not know. Experience is the best teacher. It is how we come through all the crises of life that will let us and others know how large God is in our lives. He is larger than what happened to me and you. Never allow yourself to get bogged down in hurt or anger over anything that has happened to you. It will become like cancer eating away at your mind and your body if you continue to hold on to it. Remember, give no place to the devil. Shake off anything that binds you, so it just becomes a story you tell, rather than the story you dwell on and live in day after day, rehashing it over and over. Let it go, now and forever. Release your story for the healing of yourself and others.

Oh, how He loves you and me!

POT-SMOKING DAYS

AN AUDIBLE VOICE

I was saved at the age of thirteen. For those of you who do not know what that means, it means that at thirteen, I totally surrendered my heart and life to Jesus Christ. I fell in love with Jesus and wanted to do everything I could at that age to serve Him. It was a life-changing experience. It was something I had never experienced before, and I knew it was genuine. There was something special about my relationship with the Lord. I felt special. I know everyone is special, and I knew in His eyes I was not any more special than anyone else, but deep down, I truly felt a unique bond with Him, even at an early age. I wondered if everyone else sensed this same awareness when they received the Lord into their heart. I knew for the first time in my life I was loved — maybe not by anyone else, but this one thing I positively latched on to. I am my beloved's and He is mine. This may have been due to all the dysfunction in our home, but for whatever reason, I found myself consumed with this newfound relationship.

We were raised in a church with a lot of do's and don'ts. As I look back, it was very legalistic. It was all I knew, so I tried to follow all the rules that I had been taught to a tee. I know I was young in the ways of the Lord as well as in age, but no matter how hard I tried, I always failed — not in God's eyes, but in my own. He never condemns us; He teaches us along the way. That is something I had to learn as I walked through this thing called life. The one thing I was aware of I never felt condemned by God — only others. Wow, that will preach!

I grew up quickly, or at least I thought I did, because we lived on a farm, and with so many siblings, I learned how to cook and clean at an early age. Milking cows, butchering hogs, helping in the soybean fields, and putting up vegetables for winter were our normal activities. I was in church every time the family went, and that was every Sunday and Wednesday. And of course there were always other events, plus revival meetings.

I was allowed to date at the age of sixteen, and after a summer of dating a young man I had met in the neighborhood, we got married — yes, at sixteen! Nothing would do for me except to get married. I just knew Jesus was coming soon, and I wanted a chance to be a wife and a mother, or at least that was my reasoning. Mother finally agreed after much persuasion. Now I cringe at the thought of being married at sixteen years old.

My husband was not a Christian, but I just knew after we married, he would see the light. Isn't it funny how we think? I would just beg him to go to church with me, because I knew if I got him to go, he would give his heart to Jesus. Well, that certainly did not happen! I guess that was the perfect world I had conjured up in my mind. We both would go to church, love God, have babies, and live happily ever after. I'm sure you know the rest of the story; he did not go to church with me. It was not a perfect world, so I finally began to slip away from going to church myself. I still loved Jesus with all my heart, but my pull to stay at home with my husband grew stronger than I had realized. Jesus became second place in my life.

Even so, I missed the Lord so much that I finally started going back to church once in a while to make myself feel closer to Him. I was under such conviction about my life and the way I was turning away from my best friend, Jesus. Jesus was the one true anchor in my life, yet I was putting Him on the back burner. I had no one to mentor me, and I certainly did not have anyone to explain about being unequally yoked in my marriage since the beginning. Mother was not the kind of mother who sat you down and loved on you and poured wisdom into your life. The only thing I can remember her teaching us well was good work ethics. I needed a mother or a mentor to lead and instruct me. My mother and I were never close, so I was pretty much on my own to learn the hard way. And it certainly seemed like I had mastered the hard road.

My husband and I began to smoke some marijuana occasionally, and then we progressed to doing it more often. We even grew some for our personal use since I had a green thumb, and by doing this, we would not have to purchase it. I was in my mid-twenties now with two children, and life was not turning out like anything I had expected. All my dreams of the two of us serving the Lord together were never going to happen. Reality had set in. It seemed as if I were going into a dark hole with so many heartaches and disappointments. I was at the end of my rope, not finding any fulfillment in anything we did. Life carried on as usual, month after month. The boys were excelling in sports and doing well in school. All seemed well on the outside, yet I was constantly yearning for fellowship with my Jesus. I started to go back to church, but since it was a small town and an even smaller church, I could not bear the do's and don'ts again, and so I stayed away. Over and over I would rehash things in my mind, and I felt so very lost. Was this my life? Was this all I would wake up to in years to come? I had no hope!

I would cry a lot, not even knowing why I was crying. The one thing I did know was that I did not like my life the way it was going. I wanted to change every part of this old pattern we were stuck in. But how? But when? I prayed, but no answers came.

One morning I decided I really wanted to be with Jesus. I wanted to have His full attention with me. I could not go to the church because they would judge me, but I needed Him more than ever. I needed Him, not other people at this point. I needed to sense His presence. I really wanted to run away, but there was no place to go. What was I to do?

I rolled a large joint and put it in my pocket. I walked down to the creek just beside my house and sat on a hill that overlooked a swamp bottom. I could hear the sounds of the morning, and they were soothing to my soul. Nature has always soothed me. Yes, this would be a quiet place to be alone with the Lord. As I began to smoke my joint, tears began to fall down my cheeks. I could sense I was in the presence of the Lord, not because I was smoking a joint and high, but because I had given Him access to my heart again. Before, I was closed; now I was open. I felt a warm blanket of love fall over me. It was that familiar warmth you feel when it's just you and Jesus. With no one watching and no one judging, I could be real and pour out my heart. Out under the open sky I could feel how large He was and how small I was. I had missed my best friend Jesus, the one who had been my anchor since I was thirteen. I was the one who had chosen to pull away, not Him. I had only given Him fragments of myself, and I knew He had missed me, also.

I began to weep harder as I took another hit of my joint. I told the Lord I just couldn't do this any longer. It was all too hard. I wept at who and what I had become. I prayed, saying, "Lord, I want more of You and a better life, but I feel stuck in the country, raising bird dogs, raising children, lonely, still smoking dope and not serving You" — and the shame was more than I could bear.

At that moment I heard an audible voice say, "Geneva, I want you. I want you just like you are." It startled me. I looked around and saw no one, but I knew the Lord was there with me on that hillside. It was the most overwhelming unconditional love I had ever felt. I responded to Him and said, "But Lord, I am high as a kite on pot." He said again, "I want you, and I love you just like you are; just come to Me." At that moment I was in His arms. He was reassuring me of His love for me. I basked in the moment of His love because it was good and pure. It was something I had yearned for again in my life, and I did not want to lose that moment. I did not want to get up and go back to the cares of life and the old ways.

After that Si-Fi God encounter moment, I knew I was back in right standing with my Lord, and I did not have to be anything for Him except available, and He would take care of the rest. What a powerful thought to know you are so loved, in spite of every sin you have committed. I was always harder on myself than Jesus was with me. He is always waiting with open arms for us to run into. Sometimes we need to be at the end of our rope to get to the next step. I knew I needed a change in my life, and Jesus knew I needed to change, also. I could feel the gentleness of His spirit.

This was not the best life that He had prepared for me. The best was yet to come. I just needed to want the change badly enough and then act on it.

My life did change a few years later. I had to make some serious life decisions that were not easy, but making those changes was the best thing I could have done for my children and myself. My husband and I divorced after thirteen years of marriage, and it was one of the hardest things I have ever had to do.

No matter where you are in life, God wants you just like you are — not perfect, but willing to change. He will clean us up as we move closer to Him. Let the Lord of Heaven be your change. He will meet you in your deepest darkest moments and make something wonderful come out of them. Just be real and share your heart with Him in your time of need.

Oh, how He loves you and me!

THE INHERITANCE MONEY

A LESSON IN OBEDIENCE AND PROVISION

Growing up, I never knew who my real father was. My oldest sister had located the man whose name was on our birth certificates, so naturally we all wanted to see him, since it had been at least twenty-five years or so since any of us had had any contact with him. We then set up a time for all of us to meet him in Macon, Georgia. I was excited to meet him since I had not seen him since I was about eight years old. In fact, that is the only time I can ever remember seeing him at all. I was too young to remember him when he was married to my mother. I had a stepfather growing up, but that did not take the place of knowing who my real father was. So naturally I had hopes this would be the day that I would reconnect with my biological father.

Once we located Doug, we decided that we three girls would meet him at a restaurant. We were pleasantly surprised at how well our meeting went with him, and we thoroughly enjoyed each other's company. It was awesome getting to know who our father was while enjoying sister time as well. We all lived in different states, so this meeting was a blessing for all of us. After lunch we went back to Doug's house and asked him questions about his late wife, since he had remarried, and about his daughter. We were all chattering back and forth, learning as much as possible about our father Doug in the short time we had for this visit.

I lived in Newnan, Georgia, at the time, so it was convenient for me to slip away for a few hours to run to Macon and visit with Doug after our initial meeting. I learned a lot about him and his one daughter and one granddaughter. Doug was a simple man and was living at poverty level. I usually brought him food for his apartment and would take him to lunch almost every time I visited because I knew he did not have the means to eat out. He so enjoyed a good meal out in a restaurant. It was a special treat for him, and I was delighted to make up for all the years we had missed as father and daughter. He was older and lonely, so I felt this was my reasonable service. Sometimes one of my sisters would meet me at his apartment and we would laugh, play games, and listen to him play the guitar and sing. It truly was a great time of reconnecting. As he sang and played his guitar, I watched him closely, and I had the strangest sense he was not my real father, even though his name was on the birth certificate. I had sensed this many visits prior to this one but kept it to myself and prayed about it. I did not have any of his mannerisms. I did not favor him in any way. Something was not right. Finally, I got up the nerve to ask him if he was really my biological father. He hem-hawed around and finally confessed that he did not think he was. He said he wanted nothing more than to be my father, but he had to be honest and tell me that there was a definite possibility someone else may be my father. We talked at length about his conclusion. He even told me who he thought my father was. I was grateful for his honesty in the matter, because I know it was hard for him to be honest when he wanted so much for me to be his daughter. I asked him if he would be willing to take a blood test to see for sure if he was my real father, and he said he would help me in any way he could. Doug had a gentle spirit, and I could see his heart was to help any of us girls in any way he could. At this point he informed me that he might not be the biological father of any of the four of us. Wow! That did not make any sense to me. A lot about my family did not make sense, but this story is not about my family tree, which by the way turns out to be more of an orchard; it was about finding out the truth. Doug agreed to get the blood test, and it was negative. It was 100 percent proof that he was not my biological father.

My heart was broken, and all of a sudden I felt very disconnected. The man I was told all my life was my father was not after all. In the months ahead we found out through blood tests that he fathered only one of my four sisters who carried his last name. However, over the past six months I had grown to love Doug as a father, and he felt the same for me as a daughter. I continued to visit him on a regular basis for the next year. He was very lonely, and I could not drop him like a hot potato since he had been as concerned as I was about the test results. He had a connection with my siblings, and I certainly did not want to sever that newfound joy. His only daughter in his second marriage did not live close to him, so they rarely saw one another. I also now felt an obligation since there was no one else to see to him when he needed groceries or doctor visits. Doug was very likeable. He was never demanding of my time and never asked me for anything, even when he needed it. He was a soft-spoken, gentle man. I guess you could say it was now my reasonable service to honor him as an older man alone with no one to care for him, so I did. We continued to enjoy meeting together, and I continued to encourage him to play his guitar as his fingers would allow. He said they had become stiff as he was getting older. We did laugh at the silliest things and had some wonderful times together. It made me think of what it must really feel like to have a father.

The following year Doug got sick. His organs began to shut down, so he went quickly. He had not been sick prior to this, so it was as if it was his appointed time to go meet Jesus. I was with him at the hospital and he never complained about one thing, even on his death bed. He looked up at me and told me how much joy I had brought him in his last days. I knew this was true, and I felt it to the vey depth of my soul. He also had brought me joy and laughter in the short time we had together. We wept together as I was watching him die. I truly believe nothing happens by chance. God is always in control, and the steps of a righteous man are ordered by the Lord. I know the Lord did not want this man to die alone without someone by his side. I had been put there for a season and a reason. He looked up at me and told me before he passed away that he had a small life insurance policy that he was leaving to me, and he was sad it was not more. I told him that was nonsense since we had only been reconnected about eighteen months. He grabbed my hand and insisted I accept this since he and his daughter Julie were estranged and had been for many years. I felt guilty even talking about this when he was on his death bed. He did not say how much it was, and I did not ask. Before I left for the day, we prayed together. He asked the Lord to forgive him of anything that would hinder him from making Heaven his home. Big tears were coming down his face as I agreed in prayer. Doug died the next day. He wanted to be cremated, so I honored his request. My husband Leon, one of my sisters, and I scattered his ashes on his late wife's grave, per his request. It was a simple graveside service, just as he was simple in his life. He would have wanted it that way. His daughter did not attend.

A few weeks later I received a call from Doug's insurance company telling me I was the beneficiary of a $7,500 policy. Because it was not any larger than this and everything was verified, I did not have to go to the insurance company. They informed me I should be receiving a check in the mail for that amount. This was a huge amount for him. I am surprised he even had any insurance due to his level of poverty. The call from the insurance company made me sad as it brought back memories of our time together. I was, however, thankful for the money. Leon and I were a little tight on funds at the time, and maybe this was the provision God had for us. Leon desperately needed truck tires, and this would provide the money to purchase them. Leon was grateful.

A few days later I was in my prayer room lying prostrate on the floor and praying before the Lord. My prayer room was a small room with only a desk and a chair. It was the most anointed room in our home. I would be drawn by the Spirit to come be with Him when He wanted to share something with me I would not hear otherwise. Sometimes He has to lead me beside the still waters for His name's sake and make me completely still to really hear what the Spirit says. This special room was where all the clutter in my head ceased as I focused on my sweet Savior. This was that place. This small room was always filled with the presence of the Lord. It was so anointed I would sense the power of His presence and love every time I would even walk through the doors. Everyone needs a prayer room, even if it is a closet. There is nothing like having a prayer room. It will transform your life. Many people have a prayer room but seldom find the time to use it. Please use it, and it will become your hiding place free from the cares of this world.

As I was praying, I heard the Holy Spirit say, "Give Julie all the money. It is rightfully hers as an inheritance." Julie was Doug's estranged daughter. I almost stood straight up! I shook my head at what I just heard. Did I hear correctly: "Give her all the money"? I asked, "All of it?" I was in hopes I might hear some sympathetic voice say, "No, you can keep half of it." But instead, He said, "Yes, all of it." After I heard what the Spirit was saying to me I began to weep uncontrollably. I sensed it was for Julie. I just continued to intercede on her behalf as the Spirit led me to pray. It was as if I could feel her pain and her need to be loved at that moment. I was not disappointed about the money because money comes and goes from one hand to another. This ran a lot deeper than money. It did not matter the reason; I just needed to pray as the Lord led me to, and I knew that He would take care of the rest. All I know is I had complete peace after my prayer time, and I knew beyond a shadow of a doubt that I had to give Julie all the money.

After my time in prayer, I got up and went into our great room. I sat in a chair that overlooked our back yard, and I began to think about how to break the news to Leon, because he was counting on this money to buy tires for his truck and to have a little relief in the checkbook. He was working in his office next to the great room, so he saw me come in and sit down. A few minutes later he came out to check on me, since he knew I had been in my prayer room. He knows I usually have something to share about my prayer time, and he is always so gracious to take the time to listen. I love that about him. He gets excited in his own way when the Lord speaks to me or to us about a particular matter. He is always on board, cheering me on when it comes to the things of God. What a precious man of God. As he walked out of his office, he had an excited look on his face. He said if I had a minute, he had something he wanted to share with me. I said sure and that

I had something I wanted to share with him also. He said, "Why don't you go first?" I knew he would not like what I had to say, so I politely passed the buck and urged him to go first instead.

He proceeded to tell me that while he was doing the bills, he had found a $2,000 mistake in the checkbook to our good.

I was shocked, since Leon hardly ever makes a mistake. I don't mean this sarcastically; I just know he is very thorough and double-checks his numbers. So to find this large of a mistake had to be the Lord, especially at this exact time. Si-Fi stuff, right? I was ecstatic with joy along with him as I began to cry. He wondered what was up, because that was good news. Why would I be crying? I was actually crying because that's just like our God. He was already making a way while I was in my prayer room at the same exact time. Through my being obedient, He was already making provision. The Lord knew I had just relinquished the $7,500 to Julie, and He was already on top of it because I had said yes to Him. It was my turn now to share my news with Leon. It would not be as exciting to him as it was for me, because anyone knows when you really hear from the Holy Spirit and then act upon it there is nothing, and I mean nothing, more rewarding than to obey. God always takes care of the rest of the story. I proceeded to tell Leon what happened in the prayer room. I told him we had to give all the money back to Julie and that the Lord said it was rightfully hers as an inheritance. I saw his eyes get wide and his mouth fly open as he asked me if we could keep any of it, and I said no, none of it. He sighed a big sigh and said almost too quickly, "That's OK. God just gave us $2,000 dollars, so that is more than we had an hour ago. I know if we are obedient, we will never be without." Wow, what a man of faith. Leon never ceases to amaze me. I love his simple faith in his Lord.

Naturally we both were a little disappointed, but it quickly went away as we both knew we were doing the right thing, especially since we had heard the Lord speak in such specifics.

The next day I had to locate Julie, and I explained that Doug had left some money to me in an insurance policy. She immediately told me she thought Doug had purchased a small insurance policy with her as the beneficiary years ago, but since they had not communicated all these years, she figured he must have canceled it. I told her I had cared for him the last eighteen months and even had him cremated, and we had scattered his ashes over her mother's grave. She thanked me for everything and was shocked that I would give her any of the money at all. I told her I was shocked, too, but evidently the Lord said it was rightfully hers as his daughter. She began to cry and indicated that she was sad that she and Doug had been estranged for so long and that she was not there when he died. She said she felt guilty taking the money since I had taken care of him, but she told me she could really use the money since she was a single parent. We talked a few more minutes, but before we hung up, she asked me if she could give me some of the money. I told her that was up to her but to not to feel any guilt because all the money was hers. I reminded her of how much the Lord loved her and her daughter and this was Him making provision for them. "He wanted to bless you, Julie, and remind you of His love for you, so please give Him all the thanks, not me," I told her. That was the end of our conversation.

Later that month after we had sent her a check for the full amount, she called me back and said she was sending me a check in the mail for $2,000 and would not take no for an answer. She said it was the right thing for her to do. I accepted her gracious gift and told her thank you. It was another $2,000 provision for us. Yep! That's our God. God is forever faithful. He is the way-maker.

These are Si-Fi moments I would not trade for anything. This was never about the money to begin with. Money was involved, but it was about where my heart was. This was the Holy Spirit wanting to know if I would I give up this money even when we needed it. Would I be obedient to the voice of the Lord? I would have done it even if it had been a hundred thousand dollars. It was not mine to have in the first place. These are just earthly possessions. Obedience is eternal to me. This is Kingdom stuff we are talking about.

When the Holy Spirit requires something of us that seems out of our comfort zone, just let it happen, because unless it is out of our comfort zone there will be nothing required of us that stretches us. I love being stretched in the things of the Lord. At the time it is very uncomfortable, but the reward for obedience is huge. It keeps me under the shadow of His wings. It keeps me in communion with Him. It keeps me in right standing with Him. It keeps my five senses in fine tune with Him. I want to hear, see, and know when He speaks that I heard correctly, then I do not want to walk in any fear as I act upon any assignment He has given me. Serving Him is the most rewarding thing on this side of Heaven. Do not ever let money stand between you and God. Money only passes through our hands for a moment, and then it is on to the next project or assignment. We are only stewards of what He allows to come our way. We are the managers of a tiny portion, and God sees how we manage and the motive of our hearts. I urge you to let go and see the blessings of the Lord flow into your life and finances. God owns it all, anyhow.

Oh, how He loves you and me!

THE MIRACLE HOUSE

IT'S NEVER TOO LATE

After my mother had a stroke, our family now had to regroup. Our next task was to find a quality facility in Pensacola that we all could agree upon. With the Lord's help, we eventually agreed on one in particular that was a good match for her. Mother was right at home after a few months, as well as one can be in that situation. We knew she would adjust; it would just be a matter of time. Such a transition is huge when tragedy strikes in someone's life.

After getting mother settled, we were faced with another dilemma. Our brother Chip, who has been partially paralyzed since he was eighteen years old, had been living with my mother in her home. He did not make quite enough money to be on his own, so he and my mom shared expenses, since she was a widow. This helped both of them out tremendously.

The next step was the grueling search for a home for Chip. Mother and Chip had lived in Pensacola over thirty years, so naturally Pensacola was home to both of them. He wanted to stay in the area, so off we went looking for homes in Pensacola on a shoestring budget — and it was a really short string. My sister and I were in Pensacola for a short stay to help close on mother's house since Chip was not able to afford to stay there financially, and he certainly could not keep the place up physically with his disability. Oh, my goodness, was this ever hard. For days we crisscrossed from one side of Pensacola to another trying to find something suitable. The whole time we were driving, we prayed out loud: "Lord, please help us find something in a decent area where he would be safe." I can remember crying, asking God for wisdom for our next step and the right home to pop up for us in our search. Every which way we turned was a dead-end street. The homes were more than he had money for or in such a rundown area that we knew it would not be advantageous to him. Chip trusted us to help him find a place, but if he did not like an area he would definitely speak up. Since we were on a time schedule to find him a place that we all "could agree on, we began to get on each other's nerves. We began to snap at one another and roll our eyes over each other's opinion. One would say this one was good enough while the other would say, "Yes, but … who would keep it up since Chip cannot do any outside work?" We looked at everything, including apartments and small homes.

Yikes! I wanted to run away and let the others handle it, but with my being the oldest, I had to hang in there to the bitter end. We all had to work through this process and make it work somehow. We had to have a place for our brother, now — point blank, no ifs, ands, or buts about it. We had to stay the course and keep focused. That evening when we got back to the house, I prayed earnestly. While I was showering, I leaned my head against the wall and began to cry deep sobs because we felt so lost as to what to do. I let the water beat down on my face as if it had some power to give me wisdom. I needed help to hear from the Holy Spirit. I stayed in the shower until I was beginning to shrivel up. I prayed again, saying, "Lord, You have got to help us find a house, condo or apartment." We were all exhausted. I felt like I was begging, and I know we do not have to beg the Lord for anything. He knows what is going on before we even ask. He is always way ahead of us, shifting and setting things up to accomplish His perfect will. Thank God He is smarter than all of us put together. Whew!

On our fifth and final day of the search, after looking at two homes the first thing in the morning, our countenances had fallen. We had exhausted all there was to see on the market. There were four of us in the car that day, two brothers and two sisters, and by now none of us were speaking to each other; plus, we were hungry and tired because of the stress of a week of getting the house ready for closing and a house hunt. We were disappointed in the two apartments we had scheduled to look at that morning, so we tried to talk ourselves into one of them and discussed how it might work. I knew in my heart it was not the right one, but we all had to agree as a group. Something was not right. I felt a tightness come over my chest like you feel when you are about to do something that goes against the grain.

We decided to take a lunch break and make our final decision. During lunch we all agreed to sign the papers on the apartment that we agreed might just work, although we all knew none of us were that crazy about it. Wow, was that depressing. Chip said he was not crazy about the place; however, he liked the location. He agreed he could make it work. This should have been a fun time for Chip relocating in another area in Pensacola, but we were just not feeling it. We had no other option in the time frame we were allotted. Chip had a job in Pensacola, so it was not like we could take him home with us for a couple weeks and think on it. He really needed to keep his job there, and we all knew it.

After lunch was over, we joined hands at the car and prayed over our decision, and then we got into the car to head over and sign the papers. Once we all piled into the car, we began to take turns telling each other how much we loved each other. We acknowledged that this had been really hard on us as a family with all we had to deal with in such a short time. We apologized that it had gotten so intense. While we were finishing our little speeches of love and encouragement, my phone rang. It was my friend Rhonda from Georgia. I do not usually answer my phone while I am in the middle of something, but for some reason or another I answered it.

She informed me she had gone to her Georgia lake house for some down time to be with the Lord and pray. While she was out on her back porch overlooking the lake and having her devotion, the Holy Spirit spoke to her with the most unusual words.

You really have to know Rhonda to appreciate her. When the Holy Spirit speaks to her, she just simply acts on it immediately, no questions asked. She is such a giving, loving person. I know her heart, and she lives to give. Because of this generous heart, God has blessed her so that she may be a blessing. That is just how God works. It brings tears to my eyes when I think of all the people she has so richly blessed.

As I listened to Rhonda on the phone, I began to weep. Huge tears streamed down my face. Could it be possible what I was hearing on the phone? My siblings in the car were now wondering what was going on since I was not talking but crying. They wanted to know what was wrong. Who are you talking to? Who got hurt? There was dead silence in the car.

I was intently listening to Rhonda share her encounter with the Holy Spirit on the phone. She explained that she was enjoying meditating and looking out at the lake when the Holy Spirit told her to purchase a small house on the lake as an investment property. She also said she felt the Lord say to let Chip, my brother — the one we had been searching so diligently for a place to live for the last five days — live in the house. She knew this was the Lord because she was minding her own business, reading and enjoying the morning, when all of a sudden the Spirit revealed this plan to her. She began to ponder on her assignment to make sure this was God because this was no small thing. Buy a house that she really did not need? For someone else to live in? She did not even know Chip. She had heard me talk about him because he is my brother, but she had actually never met him. Sure enough, she began to experience the kind of excitement that comes when you just know that you know you heard from Heaven and there is nothing else to do but act upon it! To top this off, she had already called Leon, my husband, to take her around the lake in search of a few homes to look at. Leon is a real estate agent at the lake, so this would be easy enough for him to do.

This was all happening so quickly. My siblings could not wait for me to finish my conversation so I could inform them what was going on. They were all just hoping this was not bad news because I was still crying. I don't think any of us could have taken anything else this week.

My last and what seemed like my only words to Rhonda (because she was doing all the talking) was, "Are you sure?" She said yes and that she was excited, and she said all this made perfect sense now that she had a grasp on everything and that the Lord wanted Chip to be close to me. I finally told her she did not have to do this, and she then proceeded to tell me I had to take this up with God, since it was His plan, not hers.

After hanging up the phone I just sat there for a moment to regain my thoughts as to what just happened. I began to tell my siblings the whole story and that Rhonda was going to buy a cabin on the lake and let Chip live there. I filled them in on all the details that I knew up to that point. They were totally amazed, as I was. They wanted to know why she would do such a thing. I told them that she has always been sensitive to the Spirit and that it was what the Holy Spirit told her to do. She knows God is the way-maker, and this was His plan to work the things out that we all had been so diligently praying for. I asked Chip what he thought about all this, and he implied he was fine with whatever we all agreed on.

We all sat in the car in awe breathing a huge sigh of relief. I think we all looked like four deer standing in front of headlights. Our eyes were wide open as we wondered what on Earth had just happened. We had been through five grueling days of house searching, with sleepless nights and a succession of rundown houses and apartments in rundown areas. We were exhausted from the yard and house cleaning to get our mother's house ready for the closing. We were also losing our patience with each other, which in itself wears you out. Wow — could all this be happening? Talk about a Si-Fi moment in time. Here we were going to sign papers at the last moment when a phone call came. I actually called Rhonda back a few hours later to be sure this was for real. As a friend, I wanted her to feel under no obligation and for her to make sure this was a God thing. After talking with her for a few minutes, I knew it was a divine appointment of the Lord to speak to her when He did, at the very moment before we signed the papers to rent an apartment for Chip. Whew, that's powerful! Chip began to embrace the idea of moving closer to his siblings, but there were a lot of details to be discussed with him about relocating in Alabama. He would have to find another job. As the day went on I began to hear an excitement in Chip's voice that I had not heard during the whole process of house hunting. He agreed this might be the very thing he needed.

Leon and Rhonda went to look at homes the next day. They looked at only three, but Rhonda found one that she thought would be great for everyone. She put an offer on it and it was accepted. They closed on it in three weeks. Chip moved in with me and relocated his job to Auburn, Alabama, where he still works today. That was another blessing, that there was an opening for him in Auburn. God was at work the whole time, setting things up that we could not see or even think about.

God is always at work in all of our lives every day. He loves being involved in every minute detail of our lives. All we have to do is ask. Chip now lives on the lake instead of a rundown apartment in a bad area. He is truly blessed because someone was obedient to the voice of the Lord. I am thankful for my friend Rhonda for being a precious handmaiden of the Lord. I know Rhonda would not want any of us to give glory to her because she realizes it was the Lord that brought all this about. She is a faithful servant, and our family loves and appreciates her.

Oh, how He loves you and me!

A MORNING AT THE BEACH

A SCHOOL OF THE SPIRIT

At one season in my life, I had been seeking the Holy Spirit to help me see things more clearly. I longed to see into the Spirit realm and not only in the natural. I wanted to be sensitive in the Spirit so I could minister to others as well as know how to intercede for the situations I was called on to pray about. I was praying for discernment, wisdom, and the gifts of the Spirit to flow more freely in my everyday walk.

For months it seemed as if I were in an intense learning process. The Lord was helping me to slow down and study what I had been hearing and seeing. He was also teaching me to be still. I am a sanguine personality type, so I have a tendency to go quickly at everything I do and think later. This causes me to miss the moment at hand. This was my season to slow down, focus, watch, and listen to my surroundings. This was a tremendous time in growing in the things of the Lord. Our Lord is always willing to meet us where we are. I wanted and needed this, and He certainly wanted to fulfill my heart's desire in drawing me closer to Him.

As I walked through this teaching from the Holy Spirit, He began to fine-tune my eyes and ears to His voice.

Things I never saw before became clearer. This totally opened up a new world for me. I began to look at and study people in a different way. I began to look into their eyes and see beyond what they were saying with their lips and hear their heart as they spoke. Whenever I would walk into a restaurant or shop, I would notice my surroundings more intently. I would see things about people. Sometimes the Lord would allow me to share with them what I saw, and other times it was just for me to know and pray silently. This is something as believers we need to work on. We need to not be so busy or in a hurry that you can't see what the Holy Spirit would show you if you would only pause, look, and listen to what the Spirit is saying. This isn't about us; it is always about others we may encounter. We should want to always look outside of ourselves and not be so self-centered. That is what true ministry is.

One day in particular I just wanted to be alone with the Lord, so I took the morning off and headed to the beach. I lived in Fairhope, Alabama, at the time, so it was a nice, quiet drive to Gulf Shores. It was a great time of the season to go to the beach. School was in, so there were no little ones scurrying around with all their chatter. I stretched out a blanket on the sand, got my Bible out, and was ready for whatever the Holy Spirit wanted to show me that day. Wow! What a quiet, pleasant morning. I was just sitting on my blanket and staring at the ocean. I picked up my Bible and began to read a few scriptures, but for some reason I could not concentrate. I laid my Bible down and just began to soak in the beauty of the ocean. Listening to the roar of the ocean and the waves slapping along the shoreline was intoxicating. The smell of the salt air was one I knew well, since I had grown up right outside of Pensacola. I began to take in deep breaths of the ocean air, and tears began to flow from my eyes. I was weeping before the Lord and aware of all His majesty and splendor. The sky, the ocean, the sand, and the quietness of the moment were almost more than I could take. I was enjoying our time together already, and I knew there was something special about this day that had been set aside to learn more of Him. How vast and huge His presence felt at that moment. How small I felt in the universe.

After a time of basking in His presence, I inquired of the Lord, "Is there anything in particular you want me to see?" I had sensed there was something he wanted to teach me today specifically. What insight might I leave the beach with today? As I had prepared to come to the beach that morning, I knew I was coming to be with the Father, and I got so excited at what I might learn. I was like a schoolgirl getting ready to see her boyfriend. I was almost giddy with anticipation.

I continued to stare at the ocean in hopes I would see something out of the ordinary. There was a large ship in the distance. I pondered on that for a few minutes and nothing came. That was not it. I prayed, "Lord, I know you want me to see something." The word "see" kept popping into my mind. I sensed I would know it when I saw it. Still, nothing came to me. I then lay prostrate on my blanket with my chin on my arms. As I looked down the beach, only a few people were in sight. A man and woman walked by me, and I studied them, and still nothing came. After a period of about an hour, I felt a tad frustrated. I wasn't trying to make something happen; I just know myself, and I also knew I was supposed to see something that morning that would be a teaching for me that particular day. I just needed to be still and wait on the Lord.

Being somewhat bored at this point, I began to watch the seagulls. Isn't that what everyone does when they go to the beach and relax? They flew in and out, swooping over me in hopes I might throw a morsel of food their way. As I began to watch them, I knew this is what I was supposed to be looking at. What was it about the seagulls? Yes, Lord, what do You want me to see? I began to watch about a dozen seagulls hang out as they stood in the sand right in front of me. I was intrigued by them as they faced the ocean standing erect as the wind blew in their faces. They were like soldiers at watch. I studied the closely. What was the Holy Spirit showing me about these birds? No matter how hard I looked, I could not see what I was supposed to see. I said, "Lord, you are going to have to help me see." Probably fifteen minutes went by to no avail; I saw nothing. I laid my head down for a few minutes while trusting when I raised it I would get it.

After closing my eyes for a few minutes, I raised my head and continued to study the seagulls. They moved around as if jockeying for position. Then all of sudden, there it was right in front of me. It was as large as day. Finally, I was seeing what the Holy Spirit wanted me to see. I began to weep uncontrollably. Right before me were the dozen birds still standing like soldiers guarding the ocean, but, and again I say but, one bird out of the twelve had only one leg. It stood out so clearly after I studied them for so long. I know they stand on one leg sometimes, but I watched them for so long I knew this one was different. The Holy Spirit whispered so softly to me and said, "Geneva, I want you to be able to see the one in the crowd that is hurt and wounded in the midst of all the others. Unless you listen and look closely, you will miss it. I have called you see the one! I have called you to be keenly aware of people in gatherings. Watch them and see what I show you. Watch my people, and I will show you the one in need. They are not always in plain view. They may be hidden in the crowd. Hurting people hide their brokenness so they appear to look like everyone else, so as to not draw attention. It is like a mask that conceals the real issue. No one wants to expose their hurts to others."

I wept. Oh, God, yes. This was so my heart, and still is today. What a lesson I received in the Spirit that morning. It is about the one that others might miss. It is about the one that will get lost in the shuffle. It is about the one that is cast down. It is about the one that needs to be loved on or prayed over that day. What a revelation of how God loves the lost and afflicted. I prayed over the one-legged seagull that very moment and asked the Lord to strengthen his one leg. I felt assured He did that very thing for me. After a time of pondering what just took place, I knew I had completed the lesson the Holy Spirit had planned for me that day. After that, I sensed a release in my heart, and I was ready to go home while filled with the goodness of God. I was energized yet humbled at what a sweet, profound parable I had just learned.

Maybe God is calling you to be more sensitive to the things that are already right in front of you. They are there right before us in our everyday lives. Just be still for a moment and wait on the Lord. Just take the time to watch, listen, and look beyond what is obvious. We all have been put here for the One. Please see the one no one else sees! Remember Jesus left the ninety-nine and went after the one.

Oh, how He loves you and me!

THE YELLOW VOLKSWAGEN BEETLE

ASSURANCE OF WHO I AM IN CHRIST

I had a dream that was so vivid and strong that it stayed with me for weeks. It was the kind of dream that I just knew had to come from the Lord. For days afterwards, the dream was as vivid as if I'd just had it the night before. Some of the scenes were somewhat eerie because I could not rightly discern their meaning. I prayed for days for the interpretation, and nothing came to me. I eventually sought counsel and the meaning became clearer.

I was captured and taken hostage by a skinhead, with a large tattoo on the back of his head. He took me to a large metal warehouse that was tucked away in the woods. It was nestled between two rather large hills, what I would call small mountains. The warehouse was well hidden off the highway and virtually impossible to see from the main road.

I do not know how I was taken hostage, because the next scene was that I was strapped to a metal table with no clothes on. My arms and legs were outstretched and strapped at my wrists and ankles. I was terrified as to what would happen next. The large building was somewhat empty with only a few boxes sitting around. I was very cold and afraid as I lay on the metal table. I looked around for any movement from the skinhead who had captured me, yet I saw no one. It was quiet and still for what seemed like a long time. As I looked to the left there was nothing, but as soon as I looked to the right he was standing right beside me. I almost jumped off the table because I was so startled, but I was strapped down. Our eyes met but no words were spoken. He then proceeded to pull a rather large knife from behind his back. He waved it in front of himself as if to taunt me. I watched the knife going back and forth. My eyes followed every move he made because I did not know his next move. What on Earth was he going to do to me? He studied me as if he were contemplating who I was and what part of me was he going to cut. My mind was swirling with fast thoughts that I did not even want see. I recognized the knife as a K-bar military knife because my husband was in the Marine Corps, so he had used this particular knife many times when we were deer hunting to skin our deer.

As he proceeded to raise the knife higher, all the fears I anticipated came to my mind. Oh, no! He is going to cut my breast off. He is going to cut me all over. I know that he saw the fear in my eyes, yet no words were every spoken. He then took his knife directly to my right thumb.

What? He was going to cut my thumb off! Crazy! Why my thumb, when he could have started in places that I did not even want to think about? He lowered the knife directly at the base of my thumb at the point where it was attached to my hand. I felt the knife begin to put pressure against my skin.

All of a sudden, out of nowhere I had this crazy idea to ask if I could go to the bathroom, so I did. I have no earthly idea how such an absurd thought could pop into my mind at a time like this. Here I am, naked, tied down to a metal table, in fear of my life, a knife pressing against my thumb, which he is apparently going to cut off, and then God knows what else, and my only response is that I need to go to the bathroom! Could this crazy thought have come from the Holy Spirit? I don't know. I have no idea where this thought was coming from. To top it off, I told him I would only be gone for a few minutes and I would be right back. He stared at me with the most hateful grin, and I was sure I had provoked him and had crossed a line. He continued to stare with glaring eyes while never speaking a word but slowly beginning to remove the knife from my thumb as if compelled against his own will. Then he began to unstrap me from the table. I could not believe he was actually unstrapping me. I felt like I had extended my life for a few more minutes. After he let me up, he waved the knife in front of my face back and forth and said, "I am watching you." I knew he was serious by the look in his eyes and the knife he was holding, but for me to delay his plan was more than I could have dreamed. "Thank you, Jesus!" At least I was free for a minute. What could I possibly do to escape? "Help me think, Lord."

While in the bathroom, I scanned the room and saw a small window. I was able to pry it open enough to crawl out and jump to the ground. I ran as fast as I could while constantly looking over my shoulder and expecting to see him chasing after me. While I was running up a hill, I was praying a car would come by to rescue me. I was still very much aware that I was totally naked and my whole body was shaking from adrenaline. I could not believe I had actually escaped. My heart was beating so rapidly. I stopped for a breath and turned around to look down at the warehouse. It was on fire. The skinhead had evidently realized I had escaped and so he had set the warehouse on fire. Why was he doing that? I knew he was evil, and now that I had escaped I knew he would kill me for sure and I would not get a reprieve next time. I had to get away. I had to run as fast as I could.

As I watched the building go up in flames, I saw something else that crushed my heart. I began to weep. Evidently, he had captured one of my sisters, and she must have been in another room. I had a brief glimpse of her face and knew she was in the building, but she was not able to escape. She was burned to death in the fire. My heart was broken. I fell to my knees and began to sob uncontrollably. Everything that was taking place was such a reality. I was captured; my sister was captured. I escaped from a crazy man who was going to cut my thumb off, and my sister died in the fire. Could this really be happening, I wondered?

I got up and began to walk down the highway while trusting a car would come to help me to safety. It seemed like no one traveled this lonely road. Lord, please let someone pass by. Yes! There it was, a car approaching me! Praise the Lord. Help was arriving. There it was, a yellow Volkswagen Beetle. I was so relieved that help was in sight. As the car approached me, I was ready to scream and tell them the story. I leaned in toward the car as they were lowering the window. I screamed and jumped back as I realized it was the skinhead driving the car. All this time I was waiting for help, and it was the man who had captured me. He glared right into my eyes; then he stuck his arm out the window while pointing his finger at me and said in a demonic voice, "I know where you are at all times, and I will be watching you." Then he sped off. I was in shock as the car drove away. I was naked, cold, and shaking all over. As I looked at the taillights go out of sight, I woke up. That was the end of my dream. Wow! What a dream. It was so vivid. I was still shaking when I woke up from the dream. I cannot ever remember having a dream this chilling. I pondered on this dream for days. Even as I write this, I feel the impact of losing a sister and possibly losing my own life in the dream.

I needed to have some closure as to what the dream meant. I can sometimes interpret dreams for others, but it was not coming to me for myself. Weeks later I shared my dream with someone I trusted in the ministry, and she gave me an interpretation that has proven to be true over the years. She explained that the thumb represented authority in the body of Christ. The skinhead represented Satan and how he could have killed me but actually wanted to kill the anointing and the position of authority I walk in. The Lord made a way of escape for me, even if it did not make any sense, like having to go to the restroom. I will never be cut off of my position in Christ. To this day I still walk in His authority and power.

This made total sense to me because around this time in my life I was stepping out in faith to a new dimension in my calling. Satan hated this. He wanted to put a stop to me, just as he wants to put a stop to whatever you have been called to do.

Do you know what I found to be a funny part of this dream? Yes! You've got it. The yellow Volkswagen Beetle. For real! Is the best Satan could do? It would be one thing if he passed by me in a Hummer, but a yellow Volkswagen Beetle — how funny! How wimpy is the devil? He tried to terrify me, but the spirit of the Lord implemented a plan of escape, and the devil bought into it. He let me go. Praise God! God always has a plan for our hope and our future.

Please know that when God calls, He equips. When God calls, He provides. When God calls, He will always make a way of escape when the enemy is at hand. I will not be cut off. I am called of God. When God calls, He will protect to see His Kingdom advance. Think about it — the enemy in the yellow VW Beetle. That is small; that is weak. He truly is weak if we see the magnitude of Christ. How big do you see the Lord as being? Satan may know where I am, as he pointed out, but he cannot touch me. I am protected by the Blood of the Lamb, and no weapon formed against me shall prosper (Isaiah 54:17).

The enemy may come at us in many forms to torment us, just like he thought he could torment me through this dream. He does not have the last word in any part of our lives. Just trust the Lord with any issue that seems to be attacking your thoughts. Give the devil no place, but continually ask God to renew your mind, and always know you are a child of God, and He will never leave you or forsake you. He keeps His promise to His children.

Oh, how He loves you and me!

WHISKED AWAY IN THE NIGHT HOUR

OUR HEAVENLY FATHER ALWAYS HEARS OUR
CRY

G rowing up, I never knew who my father was. It never seemed to bother me until my late forties. It was like out of the clear blue I had this insatiable desire to find him after all these years. I had asked my mother in my early twenties, but she could not give me a name. She was young and promiscuous when I was conceived, so I'm sure she actually did not know who he was. I just took her answer, which was, "I do not know," and tucked it away, not wanting to pursue it any further. I left well enough alone.

My husband was so sweet in wanting to help me find him if that is what I wanted to do. I had talked to an aunt, who gave me a clue as to who she thought was my father was, and he happened to be in South Carolina, so off we went in search of a man I had only heard was my father. Wild goose chase, huh? That's what we thought, but we were willing to give it a shot. I pulled up the name and address in the phone book in hopes this was the right person.

Next came the dreaded time when I had to knock on my first door and give the spiel as to why I was at their front door. My knees were shaking, since I knew anyone who approached the door would think I was crazy. I had heard stories about people who did this sort of stuff, but I never thought it would be me. I tried to make as much sense as possible with not much information to share. I had only my mother's maiden name and the name of a man who might be my father. Was I nuts? I was sincere in my story and almost apologetic for even being there.

Strike one! The first person I visited was a distant cousin to the man I was looking for, so I had gone to the wrong address. The cousin was not offering any information, and I could tell he did not want me on his doorstep. What the heck; this was a good practice run. I was so embarrassed that I asked Leon to take me back home and forget this whole nightmare. He said no; we had come too far to give up so soon. I reluctantly agreed, so we moved on to another address.

Strike two! The second address we visited was a nephew, an attorney, and he thought I was looking for money. He was very vague in all his answers, and I could tell he did not want to give me the time of day. He did give me the name of the brother of the man I was looking for, so at least I had a glimmer of hope.

I began to get excited about finding the brother, because surely he might have some information one way or another. When I arrived at the front door, a younger woman answered the door and introduced herself as a caretaker of the man of the house, and this person was the brother of the man I was searching for. I told her my story and she invited me in and introduced me to him. Guess what? He had Alzheimer's. I sat down and talked with him while hoping he might comprehend my questions.

Strike three! The only piece of information I learned from him was that the man I was looking for had died about four years earlier. I was crushed. Why hadn't the attorney nephew and the distant cousin told me this right up front? I know they were leery of me, as if they all thought I was after something. Wow, this was way too complicated. No wonder I was ready to go back home. After all this searching, the only thing that seemed remotely possible was the stories my two aunts had previous told me about who they thought my father was, and their stories matched to a tee.

Leon and I did find the gravesite of my supposed father. I cried because of the not knowing the truth. I cried because my heart was sad at there being a piece of a puzzle missing in my life. Every girl wants a daddy. I had three stepfathers but not a real father. I just wanted to know the other side of me. Surely I possessed some of his qualities as well as my mother's. I wanted to have that sense of belonging that I never had in my younger years. I was happier in my marriage to Leon than anything I could have ever dreamed of. He was definitely the man God gave me to enjoy all the days of my life, but he could not fill that small longing in my heart. I knew I had a Heavenly Father who would wipe away all my tears from any hurts that I encountered along the way so I could walk away gracefully, not knowing that part of my DNA. This man may not have even been my father. I guess it was a long shot anyway. We left South Carolina empty-handed, but I was OK.

When we arrived back home I prayed for the Lord to fill the void I had in my heart. He did. Weeks and then months went by, and I rarely thought about it. The Lord was my daddy and Leon was my husband, and it couldn't get any better than that. Life was good.

One night, months or maybe even close to a year later, I was sound asleep when I was awakened by an angel. He had no real figure to speak of; he was just a large figure. He reached his arms under my body and scooped me up while I was staring at him. His arms were large and strong as he began to lift me out of the bed. He said in a quiet but really powerful voice, "I've come to take you somewhere. I want to show you where you came from."

In an instant I was whisked away into the heavens. We were in the air for what seemed like only a few minutes. I was in his arms when he said, "We are here." I looked down and there were the twelve tribes of Israel in their camps, which made a magnificent cross from the air. I cannot express how impressive it was to see. It was not a small cross but as large as half the state of Alabama or Georgia. Their tents were huge. I knew I was in Heaven at this point, but it was all so Si-Fi, as if it were not real, yet I knew it was real. I was definitely in Heaven. I was so overwhelmed at what I was seeing, yet I said to the angel, "Oh, I'm from the tribe of Judah." I just knew I was from the tribe of Judah. He quickly replied, "No, you are from the Tribe of Levi." I was puzzled for a minute about being from the tribe of Levi. Immediately, I accepted the idea that I was from the tribe of Levi just to know where I was from. Being in the arms of an angel was more than I could comprehend. I think we hovered over the tribes for a few minutes when the angel said in his soft but forceful voice, "We must go back now." And we did. The next thing I knew I was waking up and it was breaking daylight. Talk about a Si-Fi encounter.

This was not just a dream or vision. It was for real. An angel most definitely came and lifted me out of the bed and took me to Heaven. The next morning I was awestruck over what had happened during the night. I replayed the angel's voice over and over in my head. How strong and precise. He had used just a few words and was right to the point. He did not hesitate to correct me when I stated I was from the tribe of Judah, saying, "No, you are from the tribe of Levi." I remember how he said we must go back now as if he or we would turn into a pumpkin if we were not on schedule. Maybe he had more assignments to complete that night. I don't know, but I was honored to be a part of any schedule the angel might have.

What was this all about? As I thought about this miracle from God, my only conclusion was that He wanted to let me know where I had come from since that had been my heart's cry. The Lord knew I was hurting about not having a daddy, and He wanted to bless me and let me know He heard my cry. I was special to Him, just as we all are, but He took it way further than I could have ever dreamed. He did care. He always does. He was listening to my heart saying I wanted to know my DNA. Wow, what a family tree lesson I got. I got to see my ancestors all the way back to the twelve tribes of Israel. Never in my wildest imagination could I think of anything that would touch my very soul as much as this did. An actual trip to Heaven! Who gets to do this? I did. The Lord knows what we need exactly when we need it. His timing is always perfect.

Leon and I discussed this over and over the next morning. I replayed every scene and savored every moment. I almost talked myself out of this really happening because it seemed so far-fetched, but I could not deny this astonishing event that had truly occurred no matter how hard I tried. I was there and it really, really happened.

Out of all the Si-Fi God encounters I have had, this is number one. And one of the sweetest things about all of this is I never even asked for this. It was a gift. It was bestowed upon me out of His deep love for a daughter who was hurting. Maybe you will never be escorted to Heaven by an angel, but our God is the God who sees. He sees your past hurts and the desires of your heart. He is faithful and He will bestow upon you His love in a way only our Heavenly Father can.

Oh, how He loves you and me!

THE POWER OF LOVE

A STORY DEALING WITH ANGER

Growing up, I came from a large family of eight children. I was the third oldest. There were six girls and two boys. The two boys were the youngest. As you can imagine, there was never a dull moment in our house. There was not much harmony due to many factors that kept things constantly stirred up. I trust this hopefully will be another book further down the road. My siblings got along very well with each other; it was just the parents who kept things in turmoil. When you grow up in that kind of environment, it is all you know, so I guess we were pretty normal in our way of thinking.

My mother seemed to always be angry about everything. When she was angry, she would usually take it out on one or more of us children. And to make matters worse, our stepfather liked to provoke her in his own manipulative way, which sent the situation spiraling out of control. We always walked on eggshells because we never knew what would trigger her. We definitely stayed clear of the two of them as to not catch her wrath. He was the passive one, and she was the control freak.

I do not want you to think I hated or even disliked my mother or stepfather. I truly love my mother. She herself was a product of her environment. She just never received healing from her past. All the dreams, visions, and stories in this book are true, so I want to honest about everything I say. The stories of our life make us who we are today, and that includes the good and the bad. None of us have had a perfect life. Mine may have been a little harder than for most, but I pray that my testimonies just may bring you healing through the power of the Holy Spirit. He is the restorer of all things broken. He can and will calm the troubled waters of your soul. He did it for me, and He wants to do it for you.

I truly believe the anger my mother had was a generational thing. I saw it in operation in a lot of my aunts. They were all precious women but could be lit up in a split second. That anger was passed on to us as children, and then it became our battle to deal with. Each one of us has had to deal with it in our own way. I could see the anger in my own life surfacing from time to time, and the one thing I always vowed was to never let that monster of anger win over in my life. I never wanted to be mean like my mother, yet here I was, acting exactly like her. I saw before my very eyes the thing I had feared had come upon me. With me, I would get angry for about thirty minutes to an hour and then I would be fine. I would be so ashamed of my actions after my little tantrum. I knew this was so unbecoming. I wanted to be a godly woman, and this was not the way a godly woman would act. I would cry and repent to those I had been ugly to, and you know how that goes; it was always my children or Leon. I prayed constantly for the Lord to take this ugly rage out of my life. Anger is a strange thing because you don't even know why you get angry. You just fly off the handle over the craziest things — things that a normal person would just poo-poo off. I definitely was not normal at that stage in my life, and I would be the first one to admit it. I hated what I was doing to myself and those I loved the most. I began to fast and pray more earnestly. Actually, I was almost begging for God to help me because I was growing weary of living in that old, ugly pattern of life. I always repented quickly and was embarrassed, but was I asking too much for total healing? No, I did not think so.

In Matthew 7:7, it says ask and it will be given to you. Seek and you will find. Knock and the door will be opened to you. For everyone who asks receives. He who seeks will find. And to him who knocks, the door will be opened. Wow! Boy, I was covering all the bases. I was knocking, asking, and seeking. I know my God is able to do exceedingly greater things than I could ever imagine, and I wanted total healing. It was before me every day. I was persistent in being more like Christ than more of a ranting angry woman. The one thing I did know is that He answers prayers. He saw my heart and knew my need to be restored. I was not afraid to cry out to Him and be honest. I prayed, asking, "God, please change my heart. I'm dying inside. Will You hear my cry, because everything inside of me is needing a total overhaul?"

During this time of my life, I was married to Leon. He was my friend as well as the greatest husband any wife could ever ask for. I know I was challenging, to say the least, but he always stood beside me to help me overcome all my past hurts. To this day he is my family's anchor. We have all laughed about Leon many times because we would all say Leon was like Jesus Christ ... the same yesterday, today, and forever. Steady Eddie, so to speak. No highs and lows. Always level-headed. Yes, that's our Leon, and we are truly blessed to have him in our lives.

One day I was having my prayer time in my bedroom when the Holy Spirit revealed to me that I had never felt loved. That was a strange thing to hear, so I pondered on it for a few minutes. I knew Leon loved me with all his heart because he told me every day. Leon had also been praying with me for my healing because I had asked him to pray in agreement with me. I definitely knew my children loved me, and I felt I had quite a few friends who loved me sincerely. There was never any doubt in my mind that I was loved by God. That was settled in my heart years ago. So naturally I began to question the Lord as to what it meant when he said I never felt loved. It sounded almost silly. When I was growing up it seemed as if there were too many of us to get individual love from our parents. I don't think they even loved themselves, so there wasn't much affection passed out. Our stepfather never gave us much of his time. I never knew my real father. Mother rarely said "I love you" to any of us. Of course back then parents were not as free and affectionate as today. Maybe all this in a nutshell is what the Holy Spirit was talking about when He said I never felt loved.

After sitting and meditating on this new download from the Holy Spirit, I sensed some instructions coming as well. These were instructions on what to do the next time I felt the anger well up inside me. He, the Holy Spirit, told me to go to my husband Leon and tell him to wrap his arms around me and hold me really tight and for him to keep telling me over and over that he loved me. And under no circumstances should he let me go, even if I pushed away from him. All these instructions seemed a bit strange, but I shared everything the Holy Spirit said to me. Leon's eyes got big, and he said, "Wow I can see all this coming down at a time when you are angry." I agreed with him it might not be an easy task approaching me and holding me tightly when I knew in my heart of hearts I would probably say, "Don't you touch me or even come near me."

We both laughed at the scene that could unfold, but we both agreed to try it, and no matter how much I pushed him back, he was to aggressively hold me and love on me and not let me loose. I know Leon could have prayed for me at that very moment but it would not have worked out the way it did if I had asked him to pray right then. God wanted to deal with the hurt and it was not surfaced at that moment. Timing has everything to do with the Lord and I knew it.

I knew in my heart I could not have come up with this on my own. This sounded just like something our Holy Spirit would come up with. I had been earnestly praying about my temper blowouts. This definitely sounded like some sort of plan, and — what the heck, what did I have to lose? For days later I thought about this crazy plan to make me feel loved when in fact I already felt loved. We always feel invincible, don't we? Like I said, what the heck — let's carry the plan out and see what happens. I just felt for Leon. He had me to deal with. Yikes! I could see him approaching me and me wanting to claw his eyes out like a cat. Of course we had never been violent with each other, not even a push, but here we go; I knew what we were in store for, and I was going to be a handful.

One day further down the road I was cooking in the kitchen and something had apparently triggered me to get angry before I started cooking the meal. It never made any sense when these spells would pop up. I got snappy and proceeded to slam the pots and pans around. Every time I would open a kitchen cabinet, I would slam it closed as if I were taking the anger out on something. Anger is a strange thing because it makes no sense whatsoever, but it overtakes you while you are in that place of rage.

It is like you are outside of yourself and nothing else matters at that moment. You know and feel the ugliness of it, but that's beside the point at that very minute. Most of all, you want to stop acting that way immediately, but you just can't. It has to unfold until something or someone helps you snap out of it. For some reason you feel justified in your anger. You want to act out your reasoning, however absurd it might be. As crazy as it may seem, if someone asked you why you were mad, you probably could not even pinpoint anything in particular. It is a spirit that comes over you in an instant, like a huge wave that pulls you under until it crashes at the shore and breaks up. I detest this ugly feeling. For those of you with anger issues, you know exactly what I am talking about. My prayer for you is a radical encounter with the Holy Spirit. He will lead and guide you into all truth. Ask Him and He will instruct you as He has me. He is no respecter of persons.

Upon hearing the pots and pans clanging in the kitchen, Leon walked in and just watched me for a few minutes. I knew he was watching me and that provoked me even worse. He slowly walked towards me and began to put his arms around me. I immediately swirled around and said, "Leon, no! Don't you even think about it!" He said, "Baby, remember our plan?" I told him to not touch me and to forget the plan. He closed in on me and began to hold me, pulling my back against his chest. It was as if he had poured scalding hot water all over me. I began to squirm and squirm in his arms as I tried to get loose. The more I tried to get loose, the tighter he held me. I swirled around to face him and glared into his eyes and commanded him to let me go. I even cursed at him at this moment. Leon never let go and held me even tighter. That was our plan, but I certainly wasn't on board at this moment.

He began to tell me how much he loved me. I begged him to let me go, but he said, "No, I love you, the boys love you, Jesus loves you, and you are loved by so many people." I began to cry instead of fighting. I felt my body give in and be still as Leon kept saying over and over, "I love you." Every time he said he loved me, I relaxed a little bit more. It was as if the Lord Himself were saying, "I love you." It was gentle and soothing. Just like Christ. This seemed like it went on for a long time until I had no fight left in me. I began to cry deep sobs, almost wailing. They were coming from deep within my soul. The cries got deeper and deeper until I fell to my knees on the kitchen floor. I was crying so deeply that there was snot all over my face and Leon's arm. Leon knelt with me and let me cry as deeply and as long as I needed. Something broke inside of me that day on our kitchen floor. This was the plan the Holy Spirit had for me. This was all a setup. My deliverance of the hurts from the time I was a child all the way through adulthood was the plan. A totally broken spirit was making way for the new creation God had in store for me. The hurt I had been carrying around for years was now spilled out on a kitchen floor in Fairhope, Alabama, in front of my husband and children, that were in the other room and heard everything. Yes, I received my healing that day for the Glory of God.

I never knew exactly where all the hurt and anger came from. None of us do. When I was growing up, there were so many things that I never dealt with. I'm sure it was a little bit of all the hurts and disappointments that we all so neatly hide in our suitcase of life until the Lord wants to open it up and expose all the hidden spaces. Wow! The power of love! All any of us wants is love. God is love, and He wants us to walk in the fullness of all He has for us. I was half full of what He was longing for me to experience. Now I understand what it really means to say, "My cup runneth over."

Most people never get to experience what happened to me that day. So many people are walking around with hurts from the past because they are hiding theirs in their suitcase of life just like me. Open that suitcase up and tell God all about it. God wants to love on you personally. Love sets people free. Let the Holy Spirit reveal to you any part of your past that needs to be healed. He will show you as He showed me what steps to take to receive my healing and be set free. I have never had another anger spell since that encounter with the healer, my Lord. And I definitely give thanks to my wonderful husband Leon for his love and support in listening to the Lord. I wish every woman could have a husband like Leon. He represents Christ to me in so many ways. I am truly blessed among women.

This is another God moment in time when the Spirit steps in and does what no other can do. He whispers truth into our ear and directs our path. Will you let Him direct your path in the days ahead? Take a moment before you read the next chapter and ask the Holy Spirit to reveal the areas you may need healing. He is faithful to answer our prayers.

Oh, how He loves you and me!

FIVE O'CLOCK PRAYER

INSIGHT ON WHAT TO PRAY FOR

A s an intercessor, God calls us to pray for a season on behalf of another for something specific or for certain situations He may give us insight on. You will sense a tugging in your spirit to draw away to pray on behalf of the matter at hand. It may be a one-time prayer, or you may pray for a week, a month, or as long as the Holy Spirit leads. Nothing with the Lord is iron clad except His Word. We cannot put how to pray or how long to pray into a format. Trust your spirit to guide you, and you will know when the assignment has ended because you will feel a release to move on.

I loved the church I was attending at this season of our lives. It was a great group of believers. I sensed there were some undercurrents starting to rise up among the congregation, and I knew I was to start interceding on their behalf. I was grieved over what I felt in my spirit as the dissension continued to escalate. For me it was all craziness that I thought of as high-school bickering. I am truly amazed at how serious individuals get about church issues and how they take their eyes off Jesus. Next thing you know, three, four, and now six months later they are entrenched in who is right. They can't see they are playing right into the enemy's hand. In the church experience I'm describing, individuals began to take sides. There became two camps in the church, and both were certain they were right. I know you have seen this all before.

For a period of time I made a commitment to intercede for our body of believers to be healed and a for reconciliation process to begin. I got up at five o'clock every morning and drove to our church. I had a key, so I would let myself in. I would enter the sanctuary, dim the lights, and begin my prayer time. Some mornings I walked around and around, circling all the pews. I would anoint the pulpit, chairs, offices, and actually almost anything I could anoint with oil. Other mornings I would lie prostrate on the floor near the altar and weep for a sovereign move of God over this situation. I know my Lord, and He is able to do exceedingly great things above anything I could ever ask for. If I have a heart for this body of believers, how much more does our Heavenly Father have? Yes, even more than my heartfelt prayers. Wow, that's huge.

One morning after a couple weeks of prayer, as I unlocked the door of the sanctuary, my back began to really hurt me. Even to the point of some sharp pains. This was strange since my back was not hurting at home or on the way over to the church building. I continued on with my business of prayer and worship until it was time to go home. My back was still in some pain. I usually stayed about one hour. After a few minutes down the road, all pain subsided. Thank goodness, because this was a strange occurrence.

The next morning I entered the sanctuary again and went to the front of the church and lay prostrate on the floor and began to pray. My back began to hurt so badly that I was not able to pray lying down anymore. I got up and continued to pray as I walked around in prayer with both hands holding my lower back. I immediately thought it was because I had been lying in an awkward position. I had forgotten all about my back hurting me the morning before. I stopped praying to ponder what was happening. That was strange, my back hurting like that two days in a row. Si-Fi stuff, huh? I did not receive any insight, so I went home.

As usual, the next day I arrived at the church at five o'clock in the morning. As I entered the church, my back began to hurt again. I walked around for a few minutes, praying in my prayer language and feeling no relief. Since this was the third day these pains were occurring, I knew something was up. I'd had no pains at home and none on the way to the church. It was so strange this occurred only when I entered the building. I sat on the front seat and began to ask Holy Spirit, "What do You want me to see?" There was something I needed to know about why my back instantly began to ache upon entering the sanctuary. I asked the Lord to please reveal it to me so I would know how to pray. This was not just a coincidence. The whole time I was talking to the Lord, my back was in serious pain.

Tears were coming down my face, as I knew I was in the presence of the Lord. Within a few minutes, the Holy Spirit spoke and said the backbone of this church was hurting. He said until the leadership was healed, there would be a continuous unsettling. The backbone was the leadership. I knew that spoke truth to my heart, and now I knew exactly how to pray. As the Holy Spirit gave me insight on how to pray, I wept over all the deep wounds that needed to be healed that I was made aware of.

I continued to come to the church to pray for another week. Guess what? No back pains. Meanwhile, I continued to pray for all the things I was assigned to pray for. Little by little each day, I sensed the effectual fervent prayer of a righteous person did avail much, as the word of God says. My assignment was up, and I knew God was taking care of the rest. My job was to pray — nothing more, nothing less. The Holy Spirit was faithful about revealing truth about something that needed to be brought to light. I now knew how to pray for the leadership, but the release to be at the church building every morning had been lifted. God is so faithful. The Lord did deal with some things further down the road, but that was His job, not anyone else's job.

I share this encounter as a testimony of how God can use you. As an intercessor, the Lord may give you a word of knowledge concerning someone in the room who might need encouragement. Your knee might begin to hurt when the Lord wants to heal someone's knee. You may sense a sharp pain go through your head to let you know someone is suffering from migraine headaches. Yes, trust the Holy Spirit inside you. Sure, God could do it in a split second, but He chooses to use us sometimes so it will be a testimony to others to encourage each other. God will use us to minister to others if we will let Him. Always trust the leading of the Spirit to guide and teach you exactly how and what to pray for. This kind of insight from the Lord should happen every day in our walk with Jesus if we are to be used by Him.

Sometimes things do not make sense or seem logical, but who cares? The bottom line is to promote the Kingdom, because we know our life is not our own; it is Christ's to do as He wills with each of us. Always submit yourself to the promptings of the Spirit, and you will live a life of overflowing abundance. Use the gifts the Lord has given you for the benefit of others. That is the heart of God! Let it be yours, too.

Oh, how He loves you and me!

THE PRIZE GOLDFISH

AN ENCOUNTER IN TRUSTING OUR LORD

As my husband Leon entered into his late fifties, we had an unexpected turn of events take place in our lives. He was unexpectedly let go of his job after being with this company for twenty-six years. He had been a sales manager for a Fortune 500 company. Three other older managers were also let go at this time and replaced by younger men to whom the company did not have to pay as much salary. A new corporate guru came in and wanted the bottom dollar as low as possible so he would get all the glory. It was disgustingly sad that he eliminated the older, more seasoned managers. Leon loved his job and also truly cared for the six men he had working for him.

Needless to say, we never saw this coming. They just escorted Leon into the office one day and took his laptop with some poor excuse as to why they let him go. We knew we could not fight a large company like this, so we started thinking about what our next step in life might look like. It didn't look like much without a paycheck!

We began immediately to pray about our newfound situation. We had always trusted God for everything in our lives, and we knew this would be no different. God would supply all our needs according to His riches in glory.

Leon began to send out resumes to different companies in industrial sales. Leon was smart and very knowledgeable in his field. We knew it was just a matter of time before his resume would fall into the right hands. We were trusting and praying every day that God would open another door since this one had been closed. Not so! Four months went by without one single call. Could it have been his age? What was going on? Why was no one calling? We were very frugal during these months. Leon had accumulated six weeks of vacation pay and a small severance package, but reality was beginning to set in. What were we going to do? I was working part time at a local nursery because working with flowers and landscaping was my hobby. Actually, it was to help pay for my insatiable desire to just add one more plant or bench to my garden. Having color and texture in our yard was my specialty. Flowers, plants, and texture make the heart sing for joy. Our koi pond in the back yard was one of my favorite places, as well as my prayer room, to be alone with the Lord and hear his voice. I always got excited thinking about the process of design and landscape. Seeing the final design unfold is one of the most rewarding things a gardener can experience. Wow, when I think of how God felt as He created His handiwork and then on the seventh day rested, I imagine He just might have sat down on a big boulder by a creek and listened to the rush of the water running over the rocks. He was pleased at what He saw, and it was good.

Upon not hearing anything from anyone after the countless resumes Leon had sent out, we knew something was up. Leon and I have always believed there is a reason for everything. We felt as a couple we were strong in the Lord, and our source was not in the company but in Christ. Jesus is our true source. The company was a means of income. Everything always originates with God.

Weeks continued to go by and still nothing. I fought the fear that was entering into my heart. Our situation was not improving, so I began to pray more fervently. I quoted more scriptures. Working helped keep my mind off the negative thoughts trying to bombard my mind. Anger began to set in for this company that had stolen our income and our peace. This was unfair and unjust. Even the men who had worked for Leon said this was so deceitful and unfair. Some of them even threatened to quit the company, but Leon assured them he would be fine while reminding them that they had families to think of themselves.

One night I woke up in the middle of the night in a cold sweat. I sat up in bed, and fear gripped me so hard that I was lost as to how to even pray. I began to weep so hard I was shaking. I knew this was not trusting and believing, but I did not know how to shake it. I knew God would supply all of our needs according to His riches in Glory, and I also knew to be anxious for nothing but instead, with prayer and supplication, to give thanks to the Lord. I knew all the right things to say; however, fear was overtaking me. The next day I consumed myself in the Word and began to read about Joshua on his quest to cross the Jordan. Three times in the first nine verses the Lord tells him to be strong and of good courage. Actually, in the New King James it says to be VERY courageous. That was a word I needed to chew and meditate on. Later on in the book of Joshua, the Lord raises up Gideon to save Israel from the Midianites. Gideon begins to complain to the Lord that his clan is the weakest in Manasseh and that he is the least in his father's house. And the Lord tells Gideon, "Surely I will be with you and you shall defeat the Midianites as one man." Wow! For some reason the Lord wanted me to see the word surely. I began to meditate on this one word. I looked it up in the dictionary. "Surely" means without a doubt, most assuredly, or emphatically. God wanted us to know He was with us in our time of need. He was here. I camped out in this scripture for a few days and let it really sink in. Surely God is with us in every situation. Surely God will deliver us. Surely God hears our cry. Deep down I knew this, but keeping your spirit up day after day wears on your mind. Still, I knew God's word would not return void, and SURELY our God would come through for us.

I continued to work at my part-time job, and Leon's new job was searching for employment. Still nothing.

One day after a few really pressing days of trying to keep the faith, I began to cry on my way home from work. Frustrated and weary, I arrived at home just in time to prepare dinner. I began to fry some pork chops. About halfway through my time cooking dinner, something very unusual occurred. I heard a crystal-clear voice say, "Go, check the skimmer in your koi pond. One of your prize goldfish is trapped in it, and if you don't get him out he will drown." I froze in my tracks. Did I just hear a voice say that? It was so crystal clear and precise. It was so detailed in every way, right down to my goldfish. I immediately turned the pork chops off and went to our koi pond. I opened the skimmer and sure enough there was our favorite fantail goldfish caught in the skimmer. I had chills all over me. I reached down to retrieve him and was blown away that this was really happening. He was in the palm of my hand, and as I was transferring him from the skimmer to the main pond to save his life, I heard another voice say, "Geneva, if I love this goldfish enough to bring you out here to save it, how much more do I love you and Leon, oh ye of little faith?" With that I dropped to my knees and began to weep before the Lord uncontrollably, with sobs and sobs of seeing my sweet Lord's love for us in this beautiful picture. Wow! What love. What tenderness the Holy Spirit bestowed upon me at that moment. What a sweet parable to reveal the truth of His love for us. I repented as I wept. I felt a warm embrace go from the top of my head to the tips of my toes. Everything else in that moment seemed so insignificant.

A job, money, our future all melted away. His word came to me through this whole picture, saying, "SURELY I AM WITH YOU." I felt embarrassed at my unbelief. I had always felt like we trusted Him with our lives, but you really find out what you are made of when you are put through a squeeze. I look back and I feel like I failed so miserably, but I also know the Lord used this as a teaching tool. This was the beginning of a new level of trust we had to walk through — a level of trust I would not trade for anything in this world, even though at the time I could not see the whole picture. There were no shortcuts! We all need to let our Father in Heaven be the total provider in our lives. We need to let go of what was. For us it was losing a six-figure income and learning that just maybe our trust was in things of this world and not totally in Heavenly things that mattered.

Wow! What a Si-Fi moment in time. It was a monumental moment in our lives we will never forget. Surely He is with us.

THE REST OF THE STORY

We never did get a call from the corporate world for a job. We started our own landscaping business. This was not a lawn maintenance business — just design and installation. God has provided every job to meet every need, and Leon and I are happier than ever. God always has a plan and it is usually not what we envisioned; we just have to TRUST.

Oh, how He loves you and me!

MY BACK PORCH MORNING

EXPECT THE UNXEPECTED

Early one morning I wanted to spend some quiet time with the Lord. I got my usual cup of coffee and went out on my back porch to swing. There is nothing like swinging on the back porch when nature wakes up and everything comes to life — when quietness turns into a chatter of sounds in the background, like crows cawing, a roster crowing in the far distance, and a pair of red birds beginning their morning ritual. One red bird in a distance sings to one on the other side of the yard, almost as if they are talking to each other. A group of chickadees delights in getting to come and get water from our waterfall. Just the sound of the waterfall itself is soothing to the soul.

As I began to pray and thank the Lord for His marvelous works of creation, tears began to stream down my face. I repeated over and over, "How great Thou art, my Lord and sweet Savior; how great Thou art, my Lord and sweet Savior." I just kept swinging to the rhythm of my thoughts. As I continued to swing back and forth, I was overwhelmed by the goodness of God and how faithful He is in all things. Times like these are priceless. Quiet times with our Lord feed the soul and cause our heart to soar in joy with an awesome awareness that He is ever present. As I rocked back and forth in the swing, I was in a moment of surrender in time where nothing else mattered except my one-on-one time with Him.

All of a sudden a small chickadee flew up to the swing and landed on the handrail not more than five feet away from me. I stopped swinging so as not to scare him away. How brave he was to be so close yet not flinch as he watched me. He began to sing at the top of his lungs. As you may know, chickadees are very loud birds to be so small. He was looking right at me. Our eyes met. I was as still as possible because I was amazed than he would come so close and not fly away. As he continued to sing and not be afraid, I realized something out of the ordinary was happening here. I realized he was prophesying to me through song. I was smitten when I realized what was taking place. It was totally different than just a bird singing. It was so forceful because I knew at that moment it was the Holy Spirit speaking to me. I felt a blanket of love sweep over me that was heavy with the presence of God. The love of the Lord, my Daddy's love, my heavenly Daddy's love, was so ever-present in this amazing moment. I closed my eyes for a moment as the bird continued his message to me. I could clearly understand everything he was saying as he chirped and sang. I relaxed and let it happen. Could this be happening? I opened my eyes and stared back at him, and he never took his eyes off of me, either. We both were locked in. As I opened my heart and ears to let this unfold, I realized the chickadee was giving me an answer to something I had been seeking wisdom on and had not received an answer. He was giving me direction on the exact matter I needed an answer to. Tears began to stream down my face. I sat there basking in the Lord's presence. I did not want it to end. Only God could allow such a thing to happen. He sang a minute more and then flew away.

I knew this whole setup was the Holy Spirit showing me how much he loved me and how much he loved our time together. I was open to receive that morning when I went outside to have some quiet time with the Lord. Little did I know how the Spirit would show Himself. We should always be ready to receive and not deny that He can reveal himself to us any way He chooses. That prophesying bird was sent by God. There is no other explanation for a bird sitting that close to me and then singing to the top of his lungs and never flinching as I stared him right in the eye. Please don't let your intellect interfere with the unusual ways our Lord may choose to speak and show Himself to you.

What a Si-Fi moment in time when the God of Heaven and Earth spoke through nature to reveal Himself to a woman swinging on a back-porch swing. What a glorious morning to come outside to be with my Jesus. I know He is always there and desires to be with me, but this was the coolest cup of coffee I have ever had with God. This has ranked as one of my most special times with the Lord.

As we become accustomed to giving God some quiet time, He is faithful to meet with us in return. He loves to be with His children. Look for Him everywhere and in everything! He is always right in front of us. Who knows what or when your next God encounter might be? A prophesying bird! That is powerful stuff. That is the God we serve. So majestic and creative is our Lord. We only need to open our hearts and minds to the different ways the Lord will speak to us. Never put Him in a box. He is the God of the universe, and He wants to show that side of Himself to us. Yes, this is most unusual, but nonetheless, it really happened. Think of these few incidents in the Bible. Unusual, yes, but they really happened.

+ The parting of the Red Sea, Exodus 14

+ Nebuchadnezzar's dreams and Daniel's interpretation, Daniel 2-5

+ Phillip being transported in the spirit from one city to another, Acts 8

+ Paul's baptism of the Holy Spirit when they spoke in tongues and prophesied, Acts19:6

+ Water turned to wine, John 2:1-11

+ A donkey speaking in a man's voice to restrain false teachers, 2 Peter 2:16

+ John being in the spirit and having visions, Revelation 1-22

Since the beginning of time there have been angels, supernatural healings, visions, dreams, prophets, seers. All these things were created for the Glory of God to be revealed. They are not here just so we can tell a story. Every single thing that was created by God Almighty was made to draw all people unto Him. This means He will use a talking donkey or a singing chickadee, as in my story, to get His word out to His people by any means. These sometimes uncommon encounters are the handiwork of God. He is everywhere and in everything. Can't you just feel Him when the wind blows yet you cannot see Him? Can you hear Him at the sound of the thunder roaring and the lightning striking? Can you see His handiwork when a rainbow appears? You can see Him in the sunrises and the sunsets. I could go on and on, and I could never finish what He has created for you and me to see and enjoy. He has given us eyes to see and ears to hear. Are you open to seeing and hearing Him in different ways so that He can speak to you? We see and hear Him in the large things, but what about the still places of your heart that long for something that you know is missing? Guess what? That emptiness can be filled with a genuine, not fake or phony, relationship with Jesus Christ, and that void will never go away until you feed your soul with more of Him and His presence. Do not run from Si-Fi encounters; embrace them. Be wowed by God! He wants to minister to you in more ways than you think. Let go and enjoy God. He is waiting for you right this very minute. He is the river of life.

Oh, how He loves you and me!

THE BOAZ VISION

Have you ever had a dream or vision that was so real it seemed as if you were right there in living color, truly experiencing everything that was happening? These are powerful times that our Lord sets up to reveal His plans and purposes about incidents He wants to share with us at any given time. What a privilege it is to be a part of getting a glimpse into the spirit realm for the furtherance of the Kingdom! He allows us to see into these dreams, visions, or words of knowledge, knowing we have an assignment that will follow. Our assignment may come as the need for prayer, fasting, or sharing what we have seen as the Spirit leads. However we sense our direction, it is always fascinating to see the outcome, if the Lord allows us to be a part of the outcome. As a watchman on the wall, we decree and proclaim things, even knowing that we may never get to see the end results.

I know as I speak the word forth to the four corners of the Earth, it is heard loudly and clearly. That's my job; the rest is up to the Lord.

I had a vision concerning my neighbor's daughter, Sandra. I had met Sandra a few times on their dock at their lake house. Her parents had introduced us, and from time to time I would see her with friends and family, enjoying swimming, boating, and just having a fun weekend at the lake. Our cabin was next to theirs, so naturally we exchanged pleasantries from time to time.

Sandra was possibly in her middle thirties and single. I would see her from time to time with a regular man I assumed was her boyfriend. She was breathtaking to look at. She had long, blond, naturally wavy hair, which was just as beautiful up in a hair tie with strands hanging around her face or let down shoulder length flowing in the breeze. Sometimes she would wear a cap with long, dangling earrings that made her sassy and cute. Needless to say, any guy would have been proud to have her on his arm.

One day after we walked over to their dock, my husband and I sat and visited with their whole family. We chit-chatted about many of the issues life can throw at you. I fell in love with their whole family. They were a close family, and they all definitely had a love for Jesus that was sweet and refreshing. After being around Sandra, I soon realized she was not only stunning on the outside but more beautiful on the inside. She was gentle in spirit, but she definitely had a spunkiness about her.

At different times when she came to the lake, her boyfriend accompanied her. You could tell they were serious about one another. He seemed like a very nice young man with the best intentions towards her. It was obvious. A young couple in love is always so refreshing to observe. True love is a gift from God.

The Vision

The vision occurred around 4 a.m. I was stirred in my sleep and woke wide awake. I knew something was up, so I just lay there to see if anything came to me. I closed my eyes, and after a few minutes the vision began. I saw Sandra in a large field of what appeared to be wheat. It was about waist high. It was a large field of golden reeds that looked like they were ready for harvest. The wind was blowing slightly. Sandra's hair was flowing in the breeze, slightly blowing away from her face. She was radiant in that moment. She was stroking her hand back and forth across the top of the wheat as it swayed back and forth in the breeze. I was in awe at the beauty of this scene. Sandra's beauty, her hair flowing, and the wheat swaying back and forth in the solid golden field of wheat that was ready for harvest was mesmerizing. I stared at this scene for an indefinite amount of time when a voice spoke to me. I knew it was the Lord because I had heard it many times before. It was a familiar sound. It was powerful, gentle, and right to the point. He said to tell Sandra to wait for her Boaz and not to settle for anyone other than God's best. Tell her she will know him when she sees him and when the time is right. And her Boaz would be like no other man she had ever met. That was it. That was the vision — short and to the point, but powerful.

I fell back to sleep after pondering on was had just happened. The next morning it was as vivid as when it had occurred. I told my husband about the vision and how real it was. As always, I began to ask myself if I should share this with Sandra. We lived permanently at the lake, and for our neighbors it was their second home. Sometimes it would be weeks between their visits back to the lake. Even if the parents came, Sandra didn't come on a regular basis. Oh, well, maybe one day I would share it with her if the Lord allowed. As we all know, the longer you wait to share this kind of thing, the more likely you are to find a reason not to share it, and then you begin to ask yourself if the Lord really said it or if you just thought He did. You know the story. What are the odds I would even see Sandra for a long time?

The next morning I went about my usual routine in the house, cleaning and cooking, you know the routine. Around lunch I went outside to fill the hummingbird feeders because I noticed the day before they were low. I glanced down to lake to see if any fishermen were there, and lo and behold, there was Sandra at her dock. She was floating in the water on a float snuggled close up to their dock. She was all by herself — no parents, no boyfriend. This was strange. No, actually this was the Holy Spirit setting the whole thing up. Now I had to make a decision to share the vision or not. She already had a boyfriend and they seemed perfectly happy. Hopefully she wouldn't think I was nuts. What the heck. I have done crazier things than this for the Lord. Sounds like a Si-Fi setup to me. I love this kind of thing when the Lord gets into our business. We always try and analyze what the Lord wants us to do, don't we? I knew this was definitely from the Lord, so I told myself, "Get to it, Geneva, before the mother or someone else comes down and spoils the opportunity. Let's do it."

I put my bathing suit on, walked to our dock, and got a float out of our shed so I could float over to her dock. I timidly began to paddle over to her dock while rehashing this again and knowing she would think I'm the crazy neighbor interfering in her business. As I approached her, we began to exchange some chit-chat about the weather and the lake. Eventually I started sharing the vision I'd had of her in the wee hours of the morning. I studied her for a few minutes and asked her if this made any sense to her at all. After I told her the whole story, there seemed to be a long silence that was almost deafening. Too quiet for too long, I thought. I looked at her and there were huge tears streaming down her face. She said, "Wow, this is unbelievable." She informed me she had come to the lake this weekend to hear from God. She said she had needed some time to think and pray about her future without anyone else around. "As you know, I have been dating my boyfriend for a long time now. He is a good man and he loves me dearly. I know he will be a good husband and provider," she said. "I thought he was the one for me. Maybe deep down I was settling for my mate and just wouldn't own up to it. This weekend was my time to be alone with the Lord and seek direction. I have been praying about this for a while now but haven't taken the time to listen." Sandra told me that she had decided if she didn't hear from the Lord this weekend about any specific direction, she would marry her boyfriend. "But then you have this vision and a word from the Lord saying to wait for my Boaz," she said. "Wow, this is incredible. I really needed to hear this. This is a specific direction for me that I had been in prayer about." Sandra said that she loved her boyfriend, but she had thought she would feel different when she was about to say "I do." She told me, "I should be ecstatic when I say 'I do,' and I don't feel overjoyed or any of those rapturous feelings. I don't know what I am supposed to feel about a lifetime commitment, but it should be more than this. It was like I was getting a check in my heart about our relationship. I was beginning to think it was me, not him. He's a good man." There was a quietness between the two of us for a few minutes, and then she thanked me for sharing this and being obedient to the Lord. She could not believe the Lord would show me in a vision what was going on in her life and give her a specific direction to wait for her Boaz.

My, my, my. I almost fell off my floaty! What a Si-Fi moment. She was earnestly seeking the truth, and our sweet Savior showed up with truth. I also shared with her not to just settle for her mate because God had already picked him out for her. He would fill her heart with joy, and she would be giddy with the love she had expected all along. They will be head over heels in love with one another.

We cried tears of joy together at her dock about her future, and she resolved not to be afraid to end the relationship with her boyfriend. She knew she was to move on to the next phase of her life.

I paddled back to my dock feeling totally in awe of God's love for her — so much so that He would put that vision in another person to answer her prayer. It was such a personal word for her. The Word says, "Seek and you will find." Sandra was seeking. God always knows best. God shows up for us in the nick of time. And this was definitely a time-sensitive moment. He is so interested in everything that concerns us. He loves to be right in the middle of it. Allow Him to be a vital part of your life as you watch the supernatural encounter of God work in your everyday life.

And yes, Sandra broke up with her boyfriend after our conversation. Approximately six months later she met her Boaz. They fell deeply in love, and after a year of being engaged, they were married. She was as giddy with her love for him as he was for her. It was a true love story! God's love story!

Oh, how He loves you and me!

LOST IN THE WOODS

AN ENCOUNTER IN LISTENING TO THE STILL,
SMALL VOICE OF THE HOLY SPIRIT

It was a wonderful autumn day, and the leaves had already begun to fall. I had made arrangements to spend a few days in the mountains in Rome, Georgia, with one of my sweetest prayer sisters in the Lord. It was a family-owned cabin that had been in her family for years. It was just the kind of cabin you dream of going to for a getaway. It had real logs with a huge wraparound porch nestled back in the woods. It had plenty of swings and rocking chairs for a large group, yet it was going to be just the two of us all alone on that mountain. There were plenty of old logging roads for us to walk on and explore. I could not wait. It was going to be our time to catch up on some reading, praying, walking, and enjoying the cooler weather, since it had been a long, hot summer.

One morning after we had our time of reading our favorite book, we decided to venture out for a walk. We headed out on a logging road while enjoying the fresh air and each other's company.

We chattered back and forth as girlfriends do, covering everything from our children to what God was saying to us individually at that particular season in our lives. Rhonda and I did not live close to each other, so we did not get a chance to visit as often as we would otherwise. Catching up with each other's thoughts and life issues was the fun part of our time away. Time flew by as we continued our walk. Finally we came to a crossroads, but she was a little unsure which way to choose since she had never walked this far before. She made a command decision, and we continued on. We made another decision at another crossroads and continued to walk on. After walking a long distance, she became a little puzzled as to where we might come out. We decided to continue on rather than turn and go back the way we had come.

We felt adventurous and knew we would surely come out someplace she would recognize or a main road. That never happened, but we decided what the heck, let's just walk out, no matter where it would end. We admitted we were sort of lost but not really since we knew we would come out somewhere reasonably close to the other side of the cabin. At least that is what we thought — however, after walking another thirty minutes, we came out on a paved highway. Yes! Civilization. Once again we were stumped as to which way to go, so Rhonda decided to call her friend Chuck who lived in the area near her cabin. We explained where we were to the best of our ability, since there were not a lot of landmarks on the small strip of highway we were looking at. Thank goodness he knew where we were and questioned why we had walked so far from the cabin. Of course our answer was because we wanted to and we were being adventurous. Rhonda and I felt very safe in the area her cabin was, so that was not an issue.

When she called Chuck, he was busy on a job and could not come to pick us up; however, he said he would send his son David to chauffeur us back to the cabin. Rhonda had known this family for years, and David was more than happy to come pick us up. I was grateful for the ride home because my knee was beginning to give me some issues. I had recently begun to have some problems with a torn meniscus that needed surgery, and this extremely long walk had agitated it more than I thought it would.

On our drive back to the cabin, Rhonda introduced me to David. He told us he drives that way to work every day, so this did not even put him out. We all had a good laugh about the two of us taking a few wrong turns and ending up so far from the cabin. During the ride David was sharing about his wife and children. Rhonda was asking questions and he was answering her. I was in the back seat listening to their conversation. While I was in the back seat, I heard the Holy Spirit say to me in a quiet voice to give this young man $3,000 towards a vehicle. I thought this was strange since I did not have any money on me because we were just out for a walk. The vehicle we were in was not his but his father's. David's vehicle was in the shop being repaired. He also implied his vehicle was on its last leg. He knew he was going to have to break down and get something a little more dependable. He was sharing this with Rhonda in their conversation while he drove us back to the cabin. The three of us engaged in small talk all the way back home. When we arrived at the cabin, it just did not seen quite right for me to jump out of the vehicle, interrupting their conversation, to give him money, so I let it slide. I also did not want to toot my own horn in front of them. Besides that, I did not have $3,000 cash, so I would have to write a check. In the moment it just seemed complicated, so I thanked him again, then I got out of the vehicle ahead of Rhonda while they finished their conversation. He said he was delighted to help two damsels in distress.

On the last morning of our stay, we ate breakfast and had some final reading time. As we drove off, Rhonda said she needed to make one stop before we got on the road to head back. I did not know she was supposed to meet David's father at a local diner to give him some paperwork on a project he had done for her at the cabin. We both walked in and there were David and Chuck having some lunch. We spoke to both of them, and we all talked about our excursion that week and got another good laugh. Rhonda dropped the papers off to the father, and in a flash I thought about the $3,000 I was told by the Holy Spirit to give to David. Rhonda seemed ready to go, so I let the money thing go again not to make a scene. We got into the vehicle and drove off. I felt a check in my heart that I couldn't let go about the money, but what the heck; we were already on our way so I just needed to let it go. As we drove off, I actually felt like I was being so disobedient, but I tried to shake it off. About two miles down the road I told Rhonda I needed her to please turn around and go back to the diner for a few minutes. I then told her I was supposed to give David some money and I had not obeyed the Lord. She said it was no problem, because she is always sensitive to the things of the Lord. We drove back to the diner in silence. That was strange for us because we are always chattering. I guess we were processing what had just taken place. I was trusting the Lord that they were still there finishing up on their lunch. Great! They were still there. Rhonda stayed in the car while I was on my assignment. I walked back into the diner with a check for $3,000 that I had written while Rhonda was driving. I told David the whole story about how I was to give him some money towards a car while he was so graciously taking us back to the cabin, and I was sorry for not being obedient earlier. He was blown away by what had just taken place. Naturally we hugged, and he was so grateful. I felt a weight come off my chest. Whew! Disobedience is heavy! How freeing it is to obey the Lord.

As soon as I got back in the car I told Rhonda the whole story about how the Holy Spirit spoke to me after David picked us up to give him $3,000 towards a vehicle, and the Holy Spirit had to tell me three times. Boy, am I hard-headed. Rhonda began to laugh. I asked her what was so funny. She said the Holy Spirit had told her in the car right after David picked us up on the road to give him $3,000 towards a car also. It was the exact same amount at the exact time! Now, that's Si-Fi stuff. This is the kind of stuff you just can't make on your own. Rhonda had written David a check the morning we left and left it with the papers she gave to David's father. Neither one of us knew what the other was doing. We never even discussed it with each other until we were on the road heading out of town to go back home. This is how our God works.

That day God blessed David with $6,000 towards a newer vehicle. I would have missed my blessing to give if I had been afraid to ask Rhonda to turn around. Whew! That was close.

Actually, we hadn't been lost in the woods at all. It was a divine appointment to bless David. Think about it.

- The father could not pick us up that particular day.

- David picked us up in another vehicle because his was in the shop.

- David was available to pick us up.

- He had mentioned his vehicle was on its last leg.

- Neither of us ladies knew what the spirit was saying to the other in David's car.

- What were the odds the amount was exactly the same?

- The father and son both just happened to be there eating, but we were not expecting David to be there.

- We drove at least two miles when I was challenged again in my heart to go back and do what I should have done earlier.

- Normally I do not share the amount with another person as to the amount I give. Neither does Rhonda. But this was different. It was for the Glory of the Lord to be revealed on hearing what the Spirit is saying. This was all for David to see how the Holy Spirit was at work in his life.

- We weren't lost at all. We went to the cabin with one purpose, and God wanted us to meet a need for this young family. Provision!

Sometimes when you think you are lost or things seem strange on your daily journey, just be sensitive to the Holy Spirit. Listen to what you hear. Look and see beyond the natural. Ask Him to guide your steps. Be obedient to what the Spirit says to you, even if you have to turn around. The Lord wants to bless others through you. You will be His hands extended. This is the heart of God in action.

You are never lost just on a journey of assignments. Who knows when your next unexpected God adventure will happen? It's a breath of fresh air to your soul to fulfill any assignment He allows us to be a part of.

Oh, how He loves you and me!

YOU JUST NEVER KNOW

TRUST AND OBEY

S o many times in our life, the strangest thoughts pop into our head, and we immediately say to ourselves, "Whoa! Where did that come from?" I'm sure it has happened to everyone reading this book. The next step would be to question what I will do with what I have just heard. More times than not the things that pop into our minds are just thoughts about things that we never need to act upon. It is the things that stay with us and that we can't seem to shake, or the thoughts we know are from the Lord that linger, that just maybe we need to act upon in some way or another. I would have to say this also comes with years of experience of hearing and being discerning to know exactly how to react when this occurs to us. So many times we wrestle with the idea that the Lord may want us to share the word that came to us, yet we often talk ourselves out of it because surely God would not have us to share something so direct that we may be uncomfortable. You just never know what the Spirit may prompt you to say or pray about.

The questions we must ask are whether we are available and willing to step out on a limb and share something that to us may make absolutely no sense whatsoever. But guess what? It may make total sense to the person you are sharing it with. You can never second-guess the Holy Spirit. Just listen and obey at any cost no matter how bizarre it all may seem. We have to remember we are just the messenger. God takes care of the rest.

I have become keenly aware that when I hear that voice or nudge in my heart, I am now compelled to share what I am given, because if I don't, the person on the other end misses what the Lord wants them to hear. I know I cannot come up with these thoughts on my own, so at this point the risk is up to me. I immediately know that something personal about someone was shared with me in the Spirit for a purpose and that God is at work behind the scenes, wanting me to join Him to love on His people. I am totally sold on this because this is how God works. He uses ordinary people like you and me. We have to become stronger in the Spirit and act in obedience because our flesh would like to say no. We have two choices: share what we have heard or keep it to ourselves. Of course, there will be times that we are not supposed to share what was given to us, and then we need to just pray about the situation. When you sense the Lord may want to use you to minister to someone else just yield unto the Spirit. Gently obey with a humble heart what the Lord led you to say and let Him take care of the rest.

It's kind of like *The A-Team!* I love it when a plan comes together. I love it when I'm obedient on one end and I get to share in the results on the other end of the story. The other end of the story is where God is glorified in exactly how and when He wanted to minister to an individual in a specific way. I get to see how that individual is in awe of how God loved them enough to send someone with a specific word that only God could have known about. It truly blows them away. Of course I'm always blown away at the tenderness of God to speak into someone's life in a time of need through another person. That's our Jesus!

After we moved to the lake, we needed a carpenter to build a laundry and storage room on the back of our cabin. Most of the older lake homes had absolutely no storage whatsoever. Also, most of the homes were second homes, and this was going to be our full-time residence, so we were in desperate need of space. We had been at the lake for a short time and did not know anyone there, much less a builder. After we asked around, someone gave us the name of a gentleman who did small jobs of this nature.

Lester was a friendly man, and he brought with him a couple of helpers to start our addition. We exchanged pleasantries during the day, and from time to time I would offer them a snack and something to drink. After about three weeks into the project, I was awakened by the Holy Spirit around three o'clock in the morning. As I lay there for a few minutes waiting to see what would come to me next, Lester popped into my mind, and all could see was his face. I just continued to lie still and see what came next. The presence of the Lord was heavy in our bedroom. At that moment I knew the Holy Spirit wanted to reveal something to me about Lester. I felt warm tears running down the side of my face as I thought of Lester. I sensed on overwhelming love for him that I immediately knew had to be from the Lord because I did not even really know this man, and for some reason I did not care for him after being around him for just three weeks. It had to be the love of the Lord. I actually could not wait for Him and His helpers to be done with our job and be out of there. But … God had other plans. The tears continued to flow, and I was open to whatever the Holy Spirit wanted to say. After a few minutes I heard the Holy Spirit say, "Tell Lester I love him and I miss him." It was so crystal clear, but that was all I heard. I love you and I miss you. Wow! I have had a lot of words to share with other people, but nothing quite this short and powerful. This means that Lester once had a personal relationship with the Lord. It had only been weeks into the job, but I had not heard anything from him that led me to believe he had any relationship with the Lord. In fact, quite the opposite. You see, you just never know.

My next step was to share with Lester what I had heard the Lord say. The next day I did not share anything. I just watched him at a distance to see if I got anything else to go with the first part. Nothing came to me except the same words: I love you and I miss you. Things did not work out for me to share with him for the next few days. I knew it would happen when the time was right.

A few days later, Lester came inside our home right after he had quit for the day to get paid for the week's work. I sat at the table with Leon and Lester. After Leon paid him, we had some small chit-chat about the lake, since Lester had been on the lake for many years. I sensed the conversation was almost over, and I did not want him to leave without me telling him the story, so I quickly asked him if I could share something with him before he left. Of course he said sure.

I told him the exact way it all came down. I explained how the Holy Spirit woke me up, and I described it all in detail so he could understand the full impact of what happened. I told Lester that the Lord said He missed him and He loved him. I said, "I hope this makes some sense to you, but I needed to share it with you regardless if it made sense or not."

I watched his reaction as he sat there in silence staring at the floor. It was so quiet. It seemed as if the quietness had become loud. I was waiting, but still no response came. I was thinking,

"Please, Lester, help me out." Was he thinking I was nuts? Finally, I broke the silence. I asked him if this made any sense to him. He just nodded his head up and down slowly, and then the tears began to flow down his face. These were not tears from a deep crying, but just quiet, slow, impactful tears. They were tears that came from a heart that was touched to his very soul. I told him that Leon and I did not need to know any more than what was already spoken. It was all good, I told him, and reminded him that God loved him and missed him.

Lester began to share at that moment how he had been involved with some big-name ministries years ago. He shared that he just could not stay there and beg for money to make ends meet for the church from such good people any longer. He always had thought there was a better way. It had left him empty with many unanswered questions. He left the church and drifted away from the Lord and never seemed to connect again. He said his love for the Lord never changed, but he had lost his love for the church system.

We prayed for him in the dining room and assured him we loved him and that it was evident the Lord loved him, too. He loved him enough to send almost a complete stranger to relay it to him. Oh, how He wanted Lester to know how much He loved him. What a precious moment! He could not believe the Lord would send someone to tell him that He missed him. He said he was beginning to wonder if the Lord even cared, and this reminder from Jesus made him feel special again.

We became friends with Lester and would see him from time to time around the lake. He was always in a hurry with some project he had going on. It never ceased to amaze me that every time I saw him, he thanked me for being obedient to the Holy Spirit and relaying God's love to him again.

Less than two years later, Lester took his own life. What a tragedy. You see, we just never know! I found out later Lester was dealing with some other issues in his life that he had been struggling with and could not seem to conquer. Always be obedient to the things the Lord puts on your heart. There are never any lost moments with Him. He redeems the time and is such a detailed God. Sometimes our assignments may seem silly or just too weird to explain. Who would ever think seven words would or could make a difference in someone's life? They did for Lester. The tears proved it. "I love you and I miss you." Seven words. Who knows how those words may have changed Lester's life at the end? Only God knows. All I know is that you and I are the messengers of the Lord. It is up to our Lord and Savior to take care of the rest. The next time you receive something from the Lord to share with others, please be obedient. It is never about us, anyhow; it is always about someone else. Do not withhold their blessing because you are afraid. Go and share the good news.

Oh, how He loves you and me!

THE SMOKING CHIMNEY

THE SWEETNESS OF GOD'S PROVISION

I t was a crisp, frosty morning around the middle of January. I had an early dentist appointment in Alexander City, Alabama, and the frost has not had time to thaw. The frost was heavy, which made it look like a blanket of snow. As I drove from the lake and got onto Highway 280, my mind was wandering from subject to subject thinking of nothing in particular. I was just enjoying a nice quiet drive and being alone. You know how it is when you are driving to a destination; you just get lost in the drive, and the next thing you know you are there.

As I looked over to my left, I saw smoke coming out of someone's fireplace and sighed, thinking how relaxing a fireplace can be on a cool morning. Not to mention how great it smells. The smoke was lingering a bit because there was no wind. I did get a brief smell as I drove by, which made it all the more peaceful. As I enjoyed my ride, I began to thank the Lord for the scenery and the sweetness of his presence that filled inside the car. I arrived at the dentist's office much quicker than I had anticipated this particular morning because I was thoroughly enjoying my morning drive.

After my appointment was over, I returned home to the usual daily chores that awaited me.

That night around four o'clock in the morning I was awakened by the Holy Spirit. I was instructed to take the rest of our firewood to a man in the house where the fireplace had been burning on my way to the dentist. The Lord had my full attention at this point. Why did this specific thought come to my mind? Did I just come up with this, or was this really the Lord? Maybe it was just a nice thing to do. But no, this was a little out there. How could I have come up with this? As I pondered on this for a few minutes, I replayed my trip to the dentist. I was minding my own business in my car. I was puzzled because I did not even remember which house it was. I was just driving to the dentist, not paying attention to the location of any house, much less the house that had smoke coming out of the chimney. Wow! It suddenly became so crystal clear as to what I was to do! So I lay there for a few minutes and thought about how to find that house. This was some more neat stuff God was up to. I finally fell back to sleep after figuring I would deal with this in the morning.

When I awoke in the morning, I knew I had not just come up with this on my own. I replayed all that was said to me in the night again, and it was a real assignment. I know the voice of the Lord, and this was definitely Him speaking.

Leon and I got our usual cup of coffee and sat down to enjoy the morning. I proceeded to tell him the whole story of my trip to Alex City the morning before. I told him how I had seen smoke coming out of someone's chimney but had no clue as to exactly where I had seen it and certainly did not know who lived there.

Then I told him what our assignment was: Take firewood to a house, but I cannot tell you where it is, and deliver it to someone we do not know. And why firewood? He had firewood already or I would not have seen smoke coming out of the chimney. What was the Lord up to? Was this a test of obedience?

Leon knows when I hear from the Lord, there is no dillydallying around. I'm all over it. I will do whatever I sense the Lord said. The problem with that is Leon always gets dragged into the scenario. To be truthful, he is so used to us doing out-of-the-ordinary things that he doesn't even skip a beat. He is always right there with me to see the assignments through. He agreed with me that this had to be from the Lord.

Now we were faced with the task of loading almost a cord of wood onto our truck and taking it to a destination we were unsure of. Talk about faith. We finished our coffee, and I began to feel an excitement about what would occur in the next few hours. There is an adrenaline rush when you are doing something you cannot explain, especially if it is something that came from the Lord, and you are totally acting in faith because you have no clue what the outcome will be. You are somewhat scared that you may have heard wrong and you will look like a total fool. It is like walking in the dark and you get to see the light at the end of the assignment. Crazy, huh? We both thought so.

After loading the firewood, off we went on our adventure. We laughed at this whole crazy scenario. Leon did inform me that I was the one to go to the front door after we found the house. After all, the Lord had spoken to me, not to him. I surrendered. We laughed, even though I was a little hesitant because this is not something you do every day.

Off we went toward Alex City looking for a house that I prayed would be using their fireplace again that morning. I was getting a bit anxious, and I didn't know why, because if the Lord said to take wood to this house, He would come through as always and show me which house. We began to look for smoke coming out of a chimney on the left-hand side of Highway 280. Leon said, "Baby, this is crazy." We continued to drive on. Yikes! There it was, exactly as it had been the day before. It actually was not on Highway 280 but on a small side road running parallel to 280. My heart began to pound because we were now going to have to pull up to the house, go to the door, and tell the whole story of how the Lord woke me up and told me to bring them some firewood. I said, "Lord, the things I do for you."

We pulled up to the door and sat there for a moment praying over our assignment. I then got out and walked up to the door and knocked. No one came, so I shrugged my shoulders to Leon, thinking, "Oh, well, I missed it. I must be wrong." I was ready to slither back to the car in embarrassment and call it a day, but I decided to knock once more a little harder, and I stood there waiting for any movement. A man in his middle forties finally came to the door. He had tattoos on both arms and a long ponytail. We made eye contact, and I proceeded to tell him the story of why we were here. I must have sounded like a lunatic.

There was a deep sigh and he shook his head. All of a sudden he began to cry. He was a heavyset, burly man, and I knew this was embarrassing for him. At this point Leon walked up to join us. The man asked us, "How did you know? How did you know I had no heat, and I was picking up twigs in my back yard just to make a small fire in order to stay warm?" He said he didn't have enough money to buy wood or to pay the electric bill.

I told him the Lord knew, so that is why we were here with this firewood. He wept and hugged us both. He kept saying over and over as he cried, "This has got to be God. How did you know? There is no way you could have known this." We agreed with him that God knew his need and that He loved and cared for him. We asked if we could unload the wood, and he eagerly helped us. He said only God could have put this together. The whole time we all unloaded the wood, he kept on saying, "This is a miracle. This is God."

After unloading all the wood, we prayed with him and shared with him how special he was to the Lord — special enough to wake a woman up in the middle of the night and tell her to take wood to a complete stranger. I told him this whole thing was set up by God to love on him and make provision for him. Yes, this definitely was a miracle from God for provision as a sign to him that God loved him and would always be there for him.

He was a single man who had lost his job at this time. He assured us he was a believer but had drifted away from God for different circumstances. He was now broken before the Lord and smitten with the revelation of how very much the Lord loved him. He said he actually felt special. And he was. This was a reminder that God knows and sees everything. God had missed him, and this encounter was a kiss from God to him.

Before we left, he asked us what he could do for us and we told him that he could just pay it forward to someone in need. We also blessed him with some money to help him out in some other areas. He was humbled and grateful, but actually, it was a humbling scene for Leon and me.

This story reminded me of the widow woman in 1 Kings. She was picking up sticks to prepare her last bit of food for herself and her son and after that they would die due to not having any more resources for food. But ... God had other plans. He always does.

This story of the man on Highway 280 and the story of the widow woman are part of the constant reminder of God's unlimited supply of provision to our way of thinking. God has an endless supply of firewood, food, and money to meet all our needs. Give God an opportunity to come through. What a wonderful provider He is.

Oh, how He loves you and me!

PARABLE OF THE ARMADILLOS

A TEACHING THAT REMINDED ME OF MY
AUTHORITY IN CHRIST JESUS

If you have ever lived in the South or know of anyone who does, I'm sure you have heard of armadillos. They are a pesky night critter that can destroy a yard by rooting up mulch, grass, pine straw, and even plants in search of grubs and insects. They can destroy a beautifully landscaped yard in one night. I have seen it happen many times. Since they are predominately nocturnal, it is hard to kill them unless you are willing to stay up all night with a flashlight in hopes you might see them rooting in your yard. Good luck!

We became inundated with these pests for a long season at our home at the lake. Week after week, one or more would come through and ransack our yard. Leon and I became very frustrated because we are landscapers and we enjoy and take pride in having a beautiful yard. It brings us joy to watch things mature after years of planting and transplanting until we have tweaked things to our liking. We love sharing our environment with friends and neighbors. Our beautiful yard becomes theirs as well. How rewarding it is to share the fruits of your labor for others to enjoy.

Week after week, the armadillos continued to come at night and wreak havoc, destroying flower beds and turning up all the mulch. I prayed they would leave, and to my disappointment they still came.

Leon and I decided to make war on them. Surely no armadillo was smarter than the both of us. We put out some traps, and we came up with a plan to sit up the whole night and shoot them one at a time until we saw no more sign of them coming through. We were determined, and yes we were ready for battle. Leon took first watch. He would sit with his shotgun from dark until 12:30 a.m., and I would take the second shift from 12:30 a.m. until daylight. And no, I was not even hesitant to kill one when I had the chance. We would then alternate our shifts. We killed four armadillos. That sounds great, but we continued to see signs in the yard where they were still coming through and destroying it. After a few weeks of this routine, our bodies became so tired due to not getting proper sleep that we began to fall asleep on our watch. We never did catch one in a trap, either, so we began to toy with the idea of moving into a condo — no plants or yard and no headaches. Sounded sweet to me at this point — but not really, because we enjoyed our home. Frustration set in, and we were wondering why in the world there would be such a great deluge of armadillos all at once. We knew from experience one would come in once in a while and maybe stay a day or two. He would do his thing and then go to someone else's yard. That was normal. Not this time. Those crazy pests were also enjoying the fruits of our labor. We were tired and at the end of our rope, and all the while there were still signs in the yard every morning that one or possibly two were still coming through. We decided to take a break for a week and get some good, sound sleep before making war on them again.

One lazy afternoon while I was taking a mental break from the armadillos, I decided to take some quality time just reading the Bible. I was sitting in my favorite chair that overlooks the lake, and I was watching two loons hang out in our cove. They are fascinating birds that have a most unusual cry or call. I was delighted to have them in our cove since I had only seen them a few times in this area. As I read the Word, I felt a sense of peace flood my bedroom. I love it when I take the time to read and be with the Lord because I know He is always there. What sweet fellowship we can all have if we only take the time. After I finished my reading, I decided to go to the kitchen and see what I could make for dinner that night, when halfway to the kitchen I heard the Holy Spirit speak to me ever so gently, but with an authority that I know comes from the Lord. He told me to quit looking at the armadillos in the natural realm and start looking at them in the spiritual realm instead. I froze in my tracks as I had never even thought to do that. I had done this many times in other areas, but not with the armadillos. I felt something warm go all over my body as I repeated out loud what I had just heard the Holy Spirit say. Do not look at the armadillos in the natural realm but in the spiritual realm. I immediately knew how to do this; I just had not thought this was something I could and should have applied to armadillos. Wow — what was the Lord showing me that was taking place here?

I walked outside onto the back porch, which is two stories off the ground and overlooks the lake. This is the main area where the armadillos did their most damage. All of a sudden, the anointing of the Lord came upon me. I saw what He needed me to see concerning the armadillos. The Holy Spirit was revealing to me in the spirit what I could not see in the natural realm because I was angry and all I wanted to do was shoot and kill them. The spirit reminded me I had been called to be a watchman on the wall, and he was drawing me in this next season to watch and pray like never before. He also likened the armadillos to the enemy. They come to steal kill and destroy. They come while you are asleep and when you least expect it. They catch you off guard. They attack your thought patterns, and you begin to lose focus of anything else that is more important because they have a grip on your mind. You become consumed with the enemy and not the things of God. That is the enemy's plan to have your heart and mind all tied up with the cares of life. All this was a total diversion from God. Wow! This is a serious lesson — and yes, another Si-Fi lesson.

This had been allowed to happen to bring back the focus of prayer to the task at hand. I knew I was being called to watch and pray in the near future for some specific things, and I would need to be able to rightly divide what is truth and enemy. Sometimes they are not so clear to see; that is why we must be led by the Spirit. It is like the wheat and the tares; they are side by side. I was being challenged again to not look at things in the natural but through spiritual eyes. Something happened that afternoon that resonated deep in my spirit. It was a crystal-clear revelation of the call of God on my life, especially for this season. My spirit began to explode with a fresh awareness that I know I possess as a believer in Christ. What a powerful illustration. Only God could set up such a parable to show this earthly picture and get a spiritual lesson across to me.

I began to walk back and forth across my back porch, prophesying with my arms outstretched towards the lake. As I prayed in the Spirit, I began to push back the enemy. I was pushing my arms out like pushing someone away from me. I kept pushing and saying, "Devil, no more. You have no authority here ever again. I push you back in the name of Jesus. I have been given all authority and dominion over the Earth, and no plague shall come nigh my dwelling place. That means my home, Satan. That means my property. Armadillos, you have to leave as you represent the enemy. This is my territory, not yours. Get out and don't come back."

The boldness rose up in me like fire. I sensed a heavy presence of the Lord as I declared what I was seeing in the spirit realm. I also repented for not being the watchman the Lord had called me to be.

Being a watchman is a full-time job. It is being ready to pray, intercede, and prophesy at the drop of a hat about specific things the Spirit brings to our attention.

After that, no armadillos came in our yard for at least six months. Every morning I would continue to push back the enemy. Then one night one did come in and do some really minor damage, but when we saw it, I just heard a whisper from the Holy Spirit, saying I should not slumber and get too slack because the enemy is always lurking. Stay on guard. I was humbled at His encouraging words because that one night reminded me to not let up. The armadillo did not come back the following night. I know the Lord was using the armadillos to keep me on my toes. Praise God for the wonderful way He teaches us. He knows our personalities, and that is the way He sometimes choses to teach us. He goes outside the box in his methods to teach us, just as He did so many times in the Bible.

It is so very important to look beyond the natural and see what the Spirit is showing us in our everyday walk. The Lord is faithful to allow us to see a God story in so many things if we stop and get a Heavenly perspective on what is around us. He longs to interact with us and teach us His ways — ways that go beyond anything we could ever think or imagine. These God encounters are what teach me along the way. I live for the Spirit to continually teach me by whatever means He chooses. You should, too! I encourage you to look at incidents that occur in your life as a teaching tool. God uses nature to reveal truths so many times in His word. Once you open yourself and allow the Holy Spirit to teach you in your everyday encounters, you will never be able to not look at things in the spirit realm again. It transforms your life when you let the Spirit teach profound truths in the simple nuggets of life. He longs to abide with you in all, and I mean all, facets of your life.

Oh, how He loves you and me!

PILING AFTER PILING

KEEP YOUR EYES ON JESUS AND STAY
FOCUSED

D o you know what a piling is? It is a vertical structure
driven or drilled deep into the ground below ground
level so as to secure the foundation you are erecting. It
must be strong enough to support the structure you are building.
Pilings are used on buildings or around the water. The piling I will
be referring to is one that has been drilled into the lakebed for
the purpose of erecting a boat house. It would be large enough to
house a boat and a couple of jet skis.

My friend Stephanie's home is the last house in the back
of a slough on our lake. A slough is a small finger of water that
runs off the main body of water. Her home has a lovely setting
tucked privately at the end and surrounded by trees and gorgeous
landscaping.

Her next-door neighbors decided to build a two-story boat house that would almost totally block their only view of the main body of water when they go down to the water and sit on their dock. At the first stages of the building process, all they could see were pilings, and after they finished it, they probably won't be able to see anything but the neighbors' boat house. Needless to say, they were disappointed that they would no longer have a view. We took them out on our pontoon boat to do a drive-by and look at the new boat house from the water since they had not been able to get their boat out while the pile driver was erecting the main pilings. They were shocked at how much view they had lost. No top had been put on yet, so that meant they would lose even more of their view when the project was completed.

You have to know my friend Stephanie and her husband to know they are the salt of the Earth. As disappointed as they were, they said it would be just fine and it would all work out. They knew they had two choices, one being that they could move on and not dwell on this every day while in the lake house they loved so much, or two, they could be angry every day, and resentment would build up and they would hate living there. They chose number one. Stephanie was determined to not let this boathouse steal their joy. The thing that puzzled them the most was that their neighbor-slash-friend did not even consider that the new boat house would totally block their view when Stephanie and her family were relaxing on their dock. And to this day our friends have chosen not to harbor ill feelings in their heart. What precious friends they are to us. We are blessed to have them in our lives.

Two nights later I had a dream. In the dream I saw numerous pilings. I was standing on the shoreline on a seawall and looking out at a lake. The water was deep. There were pilings in front of me too numerous to count. If I had to guess, I would say there were approximately seventy-five to a hundred of them in about a 10,000-square-foot span. I could just barely see through or around them. I was not at my house or at Stephanie's. All I know is I was standing on the shore by a seawall, and there was deep water in front of me with piling after piling. I was puzzled in the dream as to what were so many pilings were doing in one place. It was not any type of building being constructed. There was no rhyme or reason as to the way they were placed. They were just thick. I tried to look through them, and it was almost impossible to see.

As I stood on the bank and stared at the pilings, I got really quiet before the Lord. I was really still for a little while as I was waiting for anything. Then I heard the Holy Spirit say in that still, small voice that I know so well, "Be careful. Daughter, do not let your friends or others block your view." That was all I heard and saw. That was the end of my dream. Then I woke up.

After I woke up, I felt trapped with no way out and the pilings were the barrier. I looked at the clock and it was 12:23 a.m. I immediately got up and went outside and sat in my swing on the back porch. I began to inquire of the Lord as to what this dream meant because I could feel the impact of what had just taken place in the dream. I knew that it was a teaching from the Holy Spirit. I wanted to know exactly what I could glean from this. Nothing more came except what I had received in the dream. I walked over to the handrail on the porch that overlooks the water. The moon was full, and there was one extremely bright star shining in the sky. Everything was so still and calm as I looked up to the sky. I sighed deeply and knew there was a purpose for me having the dream, and I knew it was not just because I had been to visit my friends a few days before. As I waited on the Lord, I began to sense His presence so strongly. There it was again — that still, small voice that comes to you ever so gently. This is what I heard the Spirit say, "Geneva these pilings that you saw in the dream represent people in the days ahead — people who will try and block your view. Even close friends may become a Judas. Some may try and block your dreams and visions. They may try and break your spirit. Even though you may feel overwhelmed and blocked in, I have made a way of escape for you if you stay focused. Do not focus on them or their negative input because I will open doors and channels that I will allow you to walk through even when you are surrounded by the accuser. Do not lose sight of the things I have shown you, because it will not make sense to others." That was all I received at that time. I felt the spirit lift, and I knew that everything that came to me was straight from the Lord.

After that sweet word from the Lord, he reminded me of Stephanie, and that even though it appeared she was blocked in, he had made a way for her also. About a year earlier, she and her husband had purchased a small strip of property to the right of their home. It wasn't large enough to build a home on, but it was perfect to own just in case anyone wanted to buy it and put something funky on the property. It was kind of a protection for their property. Wow! What a blessing; what provision! Now after giving it some thought they may tear their sitting area down and rebuild it on that strip they purchased, giving them their view back — a new and better view. God is always looking out for us.

What a neat illustration God gave me through the pilings. God uses things in our everyday life to speak to us. No matter how many pilings are in your way, they can never hold you back. They may appear too numerous to count, but God will make a way and also make provision for you and me to carry out His plan for our lives. Just because people do not agree with you does not mean you did not hear from God. There will always be those who are for you and those who are against you. Stay the course and stay focused on your assignment, and our Lord and Savior will take care of the rest.

I do not know what lies ahead of me to have such a dream, but the Lord knows and has given me a promise that He has my back. I will stay close and listen to His voice when the accusers come. Let God arise and every enemy be scattered.

Oh, how He loves you and me!

PENTECOST 2020

THE DOVES, THE WIND, AND THE FIRE

It was a most unusual Pentecost in the year 2020. We all knew it was an appointed time in history that marked something supernatural in the spirit realm. Just as it was in the book of Acts, where the disciples were told to wait in the upper room to receive the Holy Spirit, we too were waiting for something we could not see in the year 2020. The disciples were waiting for a helper, a comforter, and in John 14:27, Jesus told them, "Peace I leave you." All of these things they could not see or touch. Jesus knew the disciples knew about Kingdom principles because they had been with Him for three years and heard His teachings. But now they needed something else to go along with the teachings they already knew. They needed power to go teach and heal in a world full of non-believers that would chew them up and spit them out without the power of the Holy Spirit. Sounds like today, doesn't it?

I took the last ten days leading up to Pentecost to fast and pray for something I could not see or touch. There was something definitely occurring during the fifty days of Pentecost. There was a shift in the atmosphere. There was an awareness of the presence of the Holy Spirit that made the air almost thick. Every time I walked outside, I could sense it in the wind. It had a different feel. The wind was stronger during these fifty days than those prior to leading up to Pentecost. I know it was the breath of God unleashing whatever needed to be done to accomplish His will for this appointed time. Even though I knew that God was unleashing something, I was fully aware that Satan was doing some unleashing of his own. I was experiencing an awareness as never before of the duality of good and evil. I felt it to my very soul. What was it about this Pentecost that made such a shift in the atmosphere? I wasn't sure, but it reminded me of a saying in the movie, *Forrest Gump*: God showed up! He always does.

The Saturday before Pentecost Sunday, I decided to go down to my dock at the lake and enjoy the afternoon. It was an extremely hot, sultry day. I took my Bible and some praise music to listen to. I had two umbrellas raised to make some shade so I was ready for a few hours of relaxing, just watching the boats go by. Times like these really make you appreciate the lake and all the benefits that come with it. Lake Martin is the most beautiful lake in the South. Of course I'm prejudiced. We are truly blessed to have a home here. After a time of enjoying some quiet time and relaxation, all of a sudden out of nowhere a strong wind came up. It began to blow so hard that I thought it was going to tear the umbrellas out of the stand. They screeched back and forth, sounding like they would break off at the base. Where was this rushing wind coming from? Until then there had only been a slight breeze. It had been the perfect day to go and relax. I never go sit at the dock when the wind is blowing since I live here and I can pick and choose the prettier days of calm weather to enjoy the water. This wind came out of nowhere. It continued to blow so hard that I decided to pack up and go to the house. I could not keep the pages open in the Bible because of the wind. The wind had my full attention. This was no fun anymore. I turned the music off, let down the umbrellas, and decided to go sit on the back porch to get off the water. There were only a few small soft clouds and definitely no rain in sight. This was puzzling. Oh well, there went my quiet time. I would continue upstairs.

Not more than fifteen minutes after I got on the back porch, the wind totally died down. There wasn't even the slightest breeze. It was totally calm again like it was when I went to the dock. This was unusually strange. I decided not to go back down to the dock again since I had already brought everything back up with me. I did not get the chance to relax once I got back to the house because I went inside and began to do a few things that needed to be done, so the incident with the wind did not cross my mind again.

The next morning was Pentecost Sunday. While sitting in my swing on the back porch, I decided to read a few scriptures. After reading for a few minutes, I paused to reflect on what I sensed was taking place on this particular Pentecost 2020. The Holy Spirit began to open my eyes to a few things that had occurred during the fifty days that I had totally overlooked as anything to do with the Spirit. I had noticed a pair of doves that had made a nest in an oak tree right off our porch during this time frame. Also, the Spirit reminded me of the strong winds that had blown during these fifty days. The wind and the doves were a part of this year's Pentecost I was supposed to see. Yes, I saw the wind and the doves, but Lord where was the fire that was spoken about in the book of Acts on the day of Pentecost. I leaned my head back on the swing and closed my eyes, then I inquired of the Lord about not seeing any fire. He said, "It is coming. I'm not finished yet. It will not look like the original Pentecost. That Pentecost was a time to empower the saints of God for the work of the ministry. This Pentecost the fire will come as a time of judgment and exposure." As I continued to keep my eyes closed, I saw hundreds of small fires all over the Earth. I felt a piercing go through my heart. I felt the impact of what I was seeing. Fires of judgment? What did that mean? Were they literal fires? After a few minutes, I knew it was not always a literal fire. It could be, but I believed the fire would come in many forms in the days ahead. Actually, it has already started. There will be fires of evil that will spread like wildfires. Hate will increase. People will be so easily deceived in these days. Judgment will increase as we have never seen it before. Do not be afraid of judgment. It is correction of the Lord. We need judgment. In fact, He already has set His hand to rearrange some major things that had to be addressed. Nations and cities had fire on them. I saw the fire of the Lord and the fire of evil that will spread like a wildfire. Judgment will come to those who will not listen in this season. God will expose the sin of the evil. Be not afraid. The goodness of God is correction. The Spirit of the Lord will increase like fire. People will come to the Lord as never before. Fires of revival will increase, but not as we have seen revival in the past. That was yesterday. This is a new era, a new season. Look for it.

I know this was a strange but profound insight this Pentecost morning. I was sad at some of the fires but rejoiced at those fires the Lord brought upon the land. Fire purges. Fire purifies. Pray for the fire to clean up cities and nations.

Wow, when I inquired of the Lord and asked where the fire was, I did not realize what I would see. The wind blew with unusual strength for fifty days and swept across this nation as a sign that God was breathing his plan into existence for this next season. The doves represented the peace he left us with and to not be afraid of the events that would happen right before our eyes, good and evil. Do not be afraid but have peace in God. The fire is not anything to be afraid of if we stay under the shelter of His wings. We need to dwell in the secret place of the most-high God. He is totally in charge of everything that happens. Not one second in time is not covered by His almighty hand. I understand that this Pentecost 2020 would be life changing in so many ways. Can you trust the Lord with me and continue to pray and see the salvation of the Lord for what lies ahead? God is always working His plan to further the kingdom.

Oh, how He loves you and me!

FOOD FOR THOUGHT

AN ENDLESS SUPPLY

I love it when incidents happen in our lives that challenge us and radically change our way of thinking. This one short story still impacts the core of my being even as I sit here and write it today. In fact I am crying right now at how extremely large this story caused me to view my Lord. May it ever be before me!

It was a beautiful weekend coming up, and I was excited my children were coming over for dinner. I love sharing food with my children at the table because the conversations usually just end up all over the place. It all begins with us talking about how great the food is and then somehow slides on to sports, hunting, fishing, children, and grandchildren, and it always ends up on politics. We are a well-rounded family, and I trust we all challenge each other. I know each and every one of you understand what a blessing family is in our lives.

As Clint, our middle son, drove up in the driveway, we were outside to greet him and his wife. We stood in the driveway as he showed us a small cannon he wanted to shoot for us. Clint was always coming up with fun things to do with the family. He loaded it with gunpowder and shot it. The recoil was tremendous, not to mention how loud it was. Thank goodness we lived in the country on seven acres at the time. We shot it a few more times before we went in to eat our dinner, and we all got a kick out of Clint's new toy.

Just before we went in to eat, we started talking about different subjects, and the price of gas got brought up. I asked Clint how much he was paying for gas right then. I was thinking it was around $3.59, which I thought was extremely high, and it seemed like it was continuing to go higher and higher. He answered so nonchalantly, "Mother, I don't even know the price of gas. I just pull up to the pump and Peabody Construction pays for it and I fill my truck up." I was shocked that he did not even know what the price of gas was. As a superintendent, Clint worked for a company that supplied his gas every week due to how many miles he drove from one job site to another. After hearing his reply to me, I just cocked my head to one side for a moment and thought about his answer. All these thoughts ran through my mind at the speed of light.

Let's just think about this for a minute.

- Clint just pulls up to the pump and never worries about the price of gas.

- Peabody is his source, so to speak. They pay the bill in full.

◆ Clint fills it up every time, so he has somewhat of an endless supply.

All of us know God is our source and that He supplies all of our needs according to His riches in Glory.

Although purchasing gas was never an issue for Leon and me because he is a good provider, it just seemed like a good topic to bring up since the price of gas had skyrocketed lately. But sometimes we forget the magnitude of that verse. God does supply all our needs according to his riches in glory. We tend to forget to let God be God in our everyday lives, like when we are simply purchasing gas or groceries. We simply forget to include Him in all areas and do not even realize we are doing it. We forget to see how large He is in all things.

For some reason or another, I was meant to really hear what Clint was saying. My ears were open to hear what the Spirit was saying to me. They were not just words that day. This was another lesson from the Holy Spirit. If Clint can pull up to a gas station and fill up and not even blink an eye at filling up his vehicle or the price of gas, how much more should I be able to do it? I have a Peabody, too, and his name is GOD! He owns it all. He is my complete source. I felt the ease of which Clint felt in the security in his company's ability to provide. He never gave it a second thought. I almost felt ashamed of the fact that I had honestly not felt that ease. That was my fault, not God's. This was a serious lesson for me on God's unlimited provision. I can now honestly say that every time I pull up to a gas station, this precious reminder pops into my head and I fill up with ease. There is no anxiety or worry about who is my source. How freeing and liberating it is to relax and trust in my Savior. I am always challenged through the incidents in my life to see how large God is.

How large is your God? It all depends on what you surrender to Him. Surrender it all. See Him in everything because He loves to take care of the smallest details in our lives.

God wants to provide for you in ways you have never dreamed of. There is nothing He cannot or will not touch in your life if you will let Him be God. He is the God who sees, and He is the way-maker. So the next time you pull into a gas station to put gas in your vehicle, remember … do not worry about the price of gas, because God is your endless supply. If we feel anything less than ease, then we aren't fully trusting Him to be our provider. If we do not trust the Lord for the smaller things in life, how in the world are we going to be able to trust Him for the larger issues? He wants to be such a relevant part of your life.

Oh, how He loves you and me!

THE POWER OF PRAYER

TRUST THE SPIRIT WHEN HE IS SPEAKING TO
YOU

One Sunday morning as we were getting dressed to go to church, I sensed a strong need to pray. As an intercessor, I don't always know what I am praying about unless after a few minutes into prayer the Holy Spirit reveals it to me. I was getting no direction on how to pray; I just knew my heart was heavy, and all I could do is cry. I definitely knew I was praying for something specific that was put on my heart to pray about, so when this happens, I just pray until I get a release. I was praying in my prayer language, as I knew this was the only way I knew how to pray correctly.

As we were driving to church, the intercession became stronger. Leon knew something was up due to the intensity of my prayers. I was trying to be cool in the car and not let Leon see how strong I sensed this prayer time was; however, Leon has seen me pray boldly in the Spirit many times and is used to me being obedient to the Holy Spirit. As we drove into the parking lot of the church, the intercession still had not lifted, so I told him I needed to stay in the car until I had a release. He went inside and I stayed and prayed for about twenty minutes until I felt I was able to go inside without crying. As I entered the foyer of the church, I felt the intercession come back strongly again. I held it back so I would not make a scene. One of the associate pastors was greeting that morning and asked me how I was doing. As soon as he finished talking to me, I broke down in tears in front of him. I was trying so desperately to suppress what was going on. He immediately asked if I was OK, and I told him the story of how intercession was heavy on my heart that morning and evidently it had not fully lifted. He immediately escorted me to his office and told me I was free to pray as long as was necessary. Once I was behind closed doors, I lay prostrate on the floor and it was as if a dam had broken. I began to weep and sob deeply, and I didn't even know why. I sensed it was for the pastor of our congregation, but I wasn't sure, so I just kept on praying even though the service had already begun. I toned my praying down so I would not disturb anyone, yet the intensity was still there. I prayed in the Spirit until the service ended. I got up and pulled myself together so I could now go around others. I did not want to talk or see anyone because I didn't want to explain what had just happened, and my eyes were swollen from crying. At times like this praying is personal and is not to be a showy thing, so I wanted to slip out without being noticed. I did just that.

Leon did not know I had gone into the pastor's office to pray, so I met him at the car instead of the sanctuary. Once we got into the car, I told him I had gone into the pastor's office and prayed more. I apologized for not being able to go into the service with him, but I needed to finish my assignment. I then began to replay the whole intercession thing and say what a strange morning this had been. He agreed. Leon also proceeded to tell me what had happened during the morning service. The head pastor had announced his heart was broken to announce he was letting two staff members go due to some things he was not at liberty to discuss. He wanted to inform the congregation as their pastor before they heard it from anyone else and for us as a congregation to be careful of the things being repeated that might not be truth. Leon said his heart was broken before the Lord that this would happen in our congregation. He encouraged everyone to be still before the Lord and pray for a trying time ahead.

Wow, that just blew me away. All of this was going on while I was in intercession in a closed room lying on my face before the Lord. This is Si-Fi stuff. This is our God in action, covering his people in love at a critical point when the body of Christ is hurting and wounded. Only God could have set this up for me to be in prayer in another room while the pastor was speaking in brokenness about something that was breaking his heart as well as God's.

Can you see the heart of God in this incident? His heart is always to cover, not expose. It is for healing. Could He have taken care of this without me? Absolutely. I was in intercession for the powers of hell not to wreck a body of believers at such a vulnerable time when the enemy could wreak havoc and cause such dissension among the staff and members. I was standing in the gap for however the Lord wanted me to pray. That is why it is so important to pray in the Spirit and not in the flesh because our flesh does not know how to pray as we should. I may never understand what all I was praying for that morning, but I was available to intercede when the prompting came, and I knew God would take care of the rest. I was praying the heart of the Father that morning for His people. And yes, He is able to do exceedingly greater things that we could never begin to comprehend, and that is exactly what He did that morning through prayer.

Have you ever felt the need to pray for something, but you had no idea what it was for? If you have, I trust you have been obedient and prayed, regardless of how you looked in the situation or what others might think of you. You are God's hands extended. You are his mouthpiece. He needs and wants us to be used by Him to expand the Kingdom through the mysteries of God, even when they don't make any sense. Prayer is communication between God and His people, and the personality of our prayer depends on how the Lord wants you to pray at that given time. Always be available for the Lord to use you at His slightest prompting. You may change history because of your prayers. Certainly, prayer can and does change all things. Our life should be a life of prayer. Without it there is no communication with our Lord. He is just waiting to hear from you so the two of you can have something uniquely special together.

Oh, how He loves you and me!

EPILOGUE

Thank you so very much for taking the time to read *Our Si-Fi God*. I trust it has ministered to you in many aspects. I know all of us have different personalities and different giftings, but we all have the same God, who is no respecter of people. He loves you and me the same, and He desires to speak personally to you and through you. He will always speak to you in a way you can understand according to your personality. My heart's desire is for you to have your own personal encounters with the Holy Spirit that will radically change the way you see your personal Savior. Is He large enough for you to see Him in multiple ways, or do you always see Him the same way? Are you stretching your imagination when it concerns the things of God? Are you around people who challenge you in the things of the Lord? When challenged with a new perspective of how the Lord might speak to you, do you draw back and say, "Oh, that's too out there," or "Gosh, that is weird"? Do you ever just sit with the Lord and wait to hear what He has to say instead of you being too fidgety and you doing all the talking? Do you long to be with Him? If He woke you up in the middle of the night, would you get up, as opposed to just turning over and going back to sleep? Are you in fear when you sense the Lord asking you to minister to someone?

Think about your answers to these questions. If most of your answers are no, this may very well be a telltale sign of why you do not have more one-on-one encounters with your Lord. Please hear me when I say the Holy Spirit wants to be with you any time you are available to be with Him. He is ready to whisper things you have been longing to hear. He wants to answer your prayers. He wants to fill your heart and life with excitement instead of despair. He wants the joy of the Lord to be your strength. He also wants to open your mind to the many ways He might want to speak to you. He is creative in His ways, and as I have said, He will speak to you in your own personality so you will clearly understand. How fun is that? You and the Lord can have ongoing conversations!

As you can see after reading this book, I am a normal person who has gone through many hardships as well as victories. I'm sure many of you have similar stories to tell where God has shown up and performed a miracle in your life. He longs for this not to be just a once-in-a-while thing but an ongoing relationship where you see and know He is always giving you insight and direction.

I am finishing this book in late October of 2020, and I truly believe in the days ahead there will be a greater outpouring of the Spirit for dreams and visions as we have never seen. The prophetic voice will increase. The seers will see things in a realm they have never seen before. The year 2020 was a year of releasing, both good and evil. No matter how bad things may look in the natural realm, God will never be outdone. He will always be victorious and shine forth, and so will His people. He is equipping His people to prophesy, discern, teach, see, and hear with an anointing that we have not walked in in days past. He is giving us 20/20 vision for the things He wants us to see. That includes you, my friend. He has called you for such a time as this, so get ready. Get ready to be bold in the things of the Lord. Stand up for truth and righteousness. Let God use you to be His mouthpiece. We need to quit thinking about what others might say about a dream you might have that is a little weird to some, or when God gives you an assignment that you are afraid of. What the heck — just do it, and let the chips fall where they may. It is better to please God than man. I promise you God will get the glory, and you will be blessed for your obedience.

I know this year has been a testing of our faith for all we have gone through with the coronavirus. This year was the year of the mouth and voice, and it appeared as if Satan wanted to shut us down by wearing masks so we could not speak. But praise God that we will never be shut down and our voices were not and will never be shut down. We are now coming back with a vengeance in the power of the one who has given us all authority in Heaven and Earth, Jesus Christ. Hallelujah! And in the days ahead, we are saying yes to our calling. We are saying yes, that this is our land and no weapon formed against us shall prosper, and every tongue that rises up against us shall be shown to be in the wrong. Wow! That's a promise from God that makes me want to shout. This is our time to be dreamers. If you operate in the prophetic, prophesy to the air. It will be heard. This is our time to be radical for our Lord. We are in the last days, and in both Joel 2:28 and Acts 2:17, it says that the Lord will pour out His spirit on all flesh, and your sons and your daughters shall prophesy, and your young men shall see visions and your old men shall dream dreams. Our Lord never does anything halfway. I truly believe this will happen in a way we have never seen before. Like a tsunami rushing in, I believe these things will occur with a boldness and a power that was reserved for these latter days. People's dreams and visions will intensify, and we will be flooded with dreamers and seers so the Word will sweep across this nation as never before for the end-time harvest. Those who prophesy will be amazed at the revelation that will be imparted to them in this appointed time, and they will have a boldness that will blow their minds, and they will know this is the Lord God working in them to proclaim His word and to be His voice in the darkest hours. It will happen just as the Lord God said through his prophets of old. Even more Si-Fi encounters will be occurring, and it will be glorious to behold.

I want to say again, thank you for enjoying these God encounters with me. I desperately wanted to share them with my fellow believers to encourage us all to be open to however the Spirit may want to speak to us. It is fun serving the Lord because there are so many benefits when we hear and obey. It opens channels that flow from Heaven that unclog our ability to see and hear. As we begin to flow in the Spirit, listening and hearing become easier. We have to grow in these things and teach ourselves these principles of Heaven.

I have prayed earnestly over this book to fall into the hands of those who may be inspired to stretch themselves. The rest is up to the Lord. I love you all, and you are in my prayers.

—Geneva

Made in the USA
Columbia, SC
12 March 2021